THE 1998
Human Rights Act
explained

**DAVID LECKIE &
DAVID PICKERSGILL**

London: The Stationery Office

Applications for reproduction should be made in writing to The Stationery Office Limited, St Crispins, Duke Street, Norwich NR3 1PD.

The information contained in this publication is believed to be correct at the time of manufacture. Whilst care has been taken to ensure that the information is accurate, the publisher can accept no responsibility for any errors or commissions or for changes to the details given.

David Leckie and David Pickersgill have asserted their moral rights under the Copyright, Designs and Patents Act 1988, to be identified as the authors of this work.

A CIP catalogue record for this book is available from the British Library
A Library of Congress CIP catalogue record has been applied for

First published 1999
Third impression 2000

ISBN 0 11 702684 0

Printed in the United Kingdom for the Stationery Office by Albert Gait Ltd, Grimsby
TJ003108 C8 11/00 9385 13903

Shaun Johnpie

The *Guide to the Human Rights Act* was written by David Leckie, a practising barrister and a member of the Human Rights Group at Hardwicke Building, New Square, Lincoln's Inn, London WC2A 3SB; Tel 0171 242 2523; Fax 0171 691 1234.

The Guide to the Convention Articles in Schedule 1 was written by David Pickersgill, a practising barrister at Bell Yard Chambers, 116–118 Chancery Lane, London WC2A 1PP; Tel 0171 306 9292; Fax 0171 404 5143.

Disclaimer

This publication is intended to be a brief commentary on the Human Rights Act 1998 and should not be relied upon by any party without taking further legal advice.

Contents

1. Introduction

1.1 The Human Rights Act 1998 ("the Act") received Royal Assent on 9 November 1998. It is not known when the Act will come into force, but it is not expected to be before the early part of 2000. The Act will have an unprecedented effect on the legal systems of England and Wales, Scotland and Northern Ireland ("UK") and has been compared to a tidal wave which will transform the legal landscape and affect every area of law.[1] The substantial increase in litigation experienced in countries which have incorporated the Convention into domestic law is likely to be repeated in the UK.

1.2 The main provisions of the Act are as follows:

- the European Convention for the Protection of Human Rights and Fundamental Freedoms ("the Convention") is incorporated into UK domestic law.

- it is unlawful for public authorities to act in a manner which is incompatible with the rights and freedoms which are guaranteed by the Convention ("Convention rights"). "Public authority" is widely defined to include a court or tribunal and any person whose functions are of a public nature.

- Convention rights can be directly enforced in UK courts and tribunals ("courts") by persons who are "victims" of a violation of the Convention by a public authority and the courts can grant such relief or remedy as it considers appropriate.

- when determining a question which has arisen in connection with a Convention right, courts must take into account Convention law, which consists of judgements, declarations and advisory opinions of the European Court of Human Rights ("the Court of Human Rights"), opinions of the European Commission of Human Rights ("the Commission") and decisions of the Committee of Ministers of the Council of Europe ("the Committee").

- all legislation must, as far as it is possible to do so, be given effect in a way which is compatible with Convention rights.

- superior courts, such as the House of Lords, Privy Council, Court of Appeal and High Court, have the power to make a "declaration of incompatibility" where they find that legislation is incompatible with the Convention. This does not affect the validity, continuing operation or enforcement of the incompatible legislation. However, it may trigger a fast-track procedure in Parliament for the incompatibility to be rectified where there are "compelling reasons" to do so.

- in respect of all Bills before Parliament, the Minister responsible for such new legislation must, prior to its Second Reading, make a written statement confirming that the provisions of the Bill are compatible with Convention rights. Where such a statement cannot be made, the Minister must make a statement indicating that the government nevertheless wishes to proceed with the Bill.

---

[1] Lord Woolf, MR, Denning Law Journal 1997, 1.

2. Background to the Act

2.1 The Convention is a treaty of the Council of Europe which was adopted on 4th November 1950 and which has been in force since 1953. The UK played a central role in drafting the Convention and was the first state to ratify it. The right of states to petition the Commission in Strasbourg was extended to individuals in the UK in 1966. At present, 40 states have signed or ratified the Convention and almost all have incorporated it into their domestic law[2].

2.2 Although there is no obligation on contracting states to incorporate the Convention into domestic law, they are required under Article 1 of the Convention to "secure" Convention rights to everyone within their jurisdiction and under Article 13 to provide for an "effective remedy" for everyone whose rights are violated. Successive governments in the UK resisted incorporation on the basis that the requirements of Articles 1 and 13 were already fully provided for under UK law and procedure.

2.3 However, there was a growing concern about the extent to which the UK was meeting its obligations under the Convention. Such concern was underlined by the fact that the UK has been found to have violated Convention rights in over 50 cases before the Court of Human Rights. It was against this background that incorporation of the Convention became part of the Government's policy[3].

2.4 Incorporation will ensure that both Parliament and the judiciary give full effect to the Convention in the legislative and judicial processes. In addition, as the Convention is a "living instrument", incorporation means that UK courts, through their interpretation and application of the Convention, will be able to play a part in its ongoing evolution.

3. Convention Rights Prior to the Act

3.1 As the Convention is an international treaty, both Parliament and the judiciary have always been bound to observe and give effect to it. However, prior to the Act, Convention rights did not as such form part of UK law and it was not generally possible for an aggrieved party to enforce Convention rights directly in the UK courts. Although the acts of a public authority could be challenged in the High Court by way of judicial review proceedings, this was a domestic remedy which was of limited application in respect of Convention rights.

3.2 As a result, where the remedy of judicial review was unavailable, the only recourse open to an aggrieved party was to petition the Commission in Strasbourg directly. This was both expensive and slow, involving a cumbersome procedure of decision making by the Commission, the Committee and the Court of Human Rights. On

---

[2] See Table A.

[3] White Paper, "Rights Brought Home: The Human Rights Bill", October 1997, Cm 3782

average, it cost in the region of £30,000 and took five years to get a case before the Court of Human Rights.

4. Procedure Under the Act

4.1 The procedure under the Act is that persons who are "victims" of a violation of a Convention right by a public authority can bring proceedings in the appropriate UK courts or rely on Convention rights in other proceedings before such courts. Procedures will be established by rules and orders and the Act will not come into force until such procedures are in place.

4.2 The remedy of judicial review is still available and indeed the Act will almost certainly lead to an increase in the number of such applications.

4.3 Once all domestic remedies have been exhausted, it is still open to an aggrieved party to petition the Court of Human Rights. The petition procedure has been greatly simplified and improved since the Eleventh Protocol came into force on 1 November 1998. The former part-time Commission and Court of Human Rights has been replaced with a single full-time Court. In addition the decision-making role of the Committee has been abolished, although the supervisory role it exercises in the execution of judgements has been retained. This should greatly reduce the cost and delay of bringing proceedings in Strasbourg. There is no right of appeal from the Court of Human Rights.

5. Practical Effects of Incorporation of the Convention

5.1 The incorporation of the Convention will have an impact on virtually every area of law and every aspect of the legal system. Lawyers, judges, magistrates, court clerks and other officers of the court will need to develop new skills and receive appropriate training to deal with the expected increase in litigation. The extensive body of Convention law, as well as decisions of the domestic courts of other states which have incorporated the Convention, will become an integral part of UK jurisprudence. All parties to proceedings under the Act will require access to such sources of Convention law.

5.2 The administration of UK courts will have to prepare for the increased workload and corresponding pressures on resources. Not only will there be specific proceedings brought against public authorities alleging violations of Convention rights but in all other legal proceedings Convention rights may be relied upon and argued either as preliminary issues or as issues which arise during the course of the proceedings. This will not only increase the number of cases which come before the courts but will also lengthen other legal proceedings in which Convention points are raised.

5.3 The financial effects of the Act are difficult to estimate but it is clear that the cost of the increase in litigation will be significant. The Legal Aid Board currently issues approximately 5000 legal aid certificates per annum for judicial review proceedings and is likely to receive many more applications for legal aid in respect of proceedings under the Act. Public authorities, in particular, will find that the Act brings new pressures and may find that extra resources will have to be made available to deal with claims under the Act.

5.4 The Act will not come into force until the judiciary have been trained to deal with Convention cases, rules and orders have been made to provide for necessary procedures and all other appropriate arrangements have been made for the legal system to respond to proceedings under the Act.

A Plain Guide to
The Human Rights Act
1998

1998 Chapter 42

An Act to give further effect to rights and freedoms guaranteed under the European Convention on Human Rights; to make provision with respect to holders of certain judicial offices who become judges of the European Court of Human Rights; and for connected purposes.

[9th November 1998]

Be it enacted by the Queen's most Excellent Majesty, by and with the advice and consent of the Lords Spiritual and Temporal, and Commons, in this present Parliament assembled, and by the authority of the same, as follows:-

Preamble
The use of the words "give further effect to" emphasises that the Convention is an international treaty which has already, to some extent, been given effect to by both Parliament and the judiciary.

Introduction

1.– (1) In this Act "the Convention rights" means the rights and fundamental freedoms set out in-

(a) Articles 2 to 12 and 14 of the Convention,
(b) Articles 1 to 3 of the First Protocol, and
(c) Articles 1 and 2 of the Sixth Protocol,

as read with Articles 16 to 18 of the Convention.

Section 1
This section defines "the Convention rights" which are to be given effect to and makes provision for the Secretary of State to amend the Act where appropriate, in order to take account of any protocols.

Subsection (1)
The Convention, as amended by the Eleventh Protocol, is in three sections and consists of 59 Articles, many of which are of a procedural nature. The Articles which have been included in the definition of "Convention rights" are those which actually confer rights.

Protocols are additions or amendments to the Convention which may be signed and ratified by parties to the Convention. There are presently 11 protocols, although only the First, Fourth, Sixth and Seventh Protocols confer further rights. The other Protocols are procedural and have been consolidated and replaced by the Eleventh Protocol. The Act incorporates certain Articles from the First and Sixth Protocols only. The First Protocol added the rights to protection of property, education and free elections. The Sixth Protocol provides for the abolition of the death penalty.

(2) Those Articles are to have effect for the purposes of this Act subject to any designated derogation or reservation (as to which see sections 14 and 15).

Subsection (2)
Derogations are provided for in Article 15 of the Convention, which allows a state to derogate from certain Articles in times of war and other public emergencies which threaten the life of a nation. Reservations are provided for in Article 57 of the Convention, which allows a state to enter a reservation where a law in force in the state is not in conformity with a provision of the Convention. The UK currently has one derogation in respect of Article 5(3) of the Convention, relating to the prevention of terrorism, and one reservation in respect of Article 2 of the First Protocol, relating to education. These are set out in full in sections 14 - 17 and in Schedule 3.

(3) The Articles are set out in Schedule 1.

Subsection (3)
The full texts of the applicable Articles of the Convention and the First and Sixth Protocols are reproduced in Schedule 1.

(4) The Secretary of State may by order make such amendments to this Act as he considers appropriate to reflect the effect, in relation to the United Kingdom, of a protocol.

Subsection (4)
The Secretary of State has the power to amend the Act by order to reflect any changes in the UK's obligations as a result of a protocol. Under section 20, such orders are to be made by statutory instrument and cannot be made unless a draft of the order has been placed before and approved by each House of Parliament.

(5) In subsection (4) "protocol" means a protocol to the Convention-

    (a) which the United Kingdom has ratified; or
    (b) which the United Kingdom has signed with a view to ratification.

Subsection (5)
At present, the UK has ratified all of the existing protocols, apart from the Fourth, Sixth, Seventh and Ninth Protocols.

The Fourth Protocol provides for the prohibition of imprisonment for debt, freedom of movement and the prohibition of expulsion of nationals and collective expulsion of aliens. It was signed by the UK in 1963 but the Government does not at present intend to ratify it.

Following its inclusion in section 1 (1) (c) of the Act the sixth protocol which provides for the abolition of the death penalty, was signed by the UK on 27 January 1999 and will be ratified in due course.

The Seventh Protocol provides for procedural safeguards in respect of expulsion of aliens, the right of appeal in criminal matters, the right to have compensation for wrongful conviction, the right not to be punished twice and equality between spouses. The Government intends to sign and ratify it once a number of inconsistencies in domestic law have been removed by legislation.

The Ninth Protocol has been replaced by the Eleventh Protocol.

(6) No amendment may be made by an order under subsection (4) so as to come into force before the protocol concerned is in force in relation to the United Kingdom.

Subsection (6)
Where the Secretary of State amends the Act to take account of a protocol, such amendment cannot come into force until the protocol upon which such amendment is based is itself in force.

2.– (1) A court or tribunal determining a question which has arisen in connection with a Convention right must take into account any-

(a) judgment, decision, declaration or advisory opinion of the European Court of Human Rights,

(b) opinion of the Commission given in a report adopted under Article 31 of the Convention,

(c) decision of the Commission in connection with Article 26 or 27(2) of the Convention, or

(d) decision of the Committee of Ministers taken under Article 46 of the Convention,

whenever made or given, so far as, in the opinion of the court or tribunal, it is relevant to the proceedings in which that question has arisen.

Section 2
This section imposes an obligation on UK courts and tribunals to take Convention law into account when determining a question which has arisen in connection with a Convention right.

Subsection 1
Lists the various sources of Convention law which must be taken account of by courts and tribunals where they consider it relevant to proceedings. "Tribunal" is widely defined in section 21.

As a result of the Eleventh Protocol, there will no longer be any opinions or decisions of the Commission or Committee to take account of, although any such opinions or decisions made prior to 1 November 1998 must still be taken into account.

The effect of this section is that not only are UK courts obliged to take Convention law into account but they are also obliged to apply the principles of interpretation established by Convention jurisprudence.

The Convention is a treaty and accordingly must be interpreted in accordance with the international rules on the interpretation of treaties, "in good faith in accordance with the ordinary meaning to be given to the terms of the treaty in their context and in light of its object and purpose"[4].

As the Convention is "a living instrument which must be interpreted in the light of present day conditions",[5] a dynamic and evolutionary approach is taken when interpreting Convention rights. This is reflected by the fact that there is no doctrine of binding precedent in respect of decisions of the Court of Human Rights and the Court is free to depart from previous decisions, provided that there are cogent reasons for doing so.

Another fundamental principle of interpretation is that of proportionality, which means that a fair balance must be struck between the demands of the community and the need to protect an individual's fundamental rights.

Although Convention law must be followed and applied by UK courts, the doctrine of "the margin of appreciation" allows the national courts a certain degree of discretion and latitude when interpreting Convention rights, subject to European supervision. The Court of Human Rights has recognised that a national court is better placed than an international court to evaluate local needs and conditions and take account of the "vital forces" of their country[6].

The sources of Convention law referred to in this subsection can be found in a number of publications, such as the European Human Rights Reports, Decisions and Reports, Commonwealth Cases, International Human Rights Reports and the European Human Rights Review. They can also be found on the following websites:

Court of Human rights: *http://www.dhcour.coe.fr*

Commission: *http://www.dhcommhr.coe.fr*

---

[4] *Vienna Convention on the Law of Treaties 1969, Article 31.*

[5] *Tyrer v UK A 26 (1978).*

[6] *Handyside v UK A 24 para 49 (1976)*

(2) Evidence of any judgment, decision, declaration or opinion of which account may have to be taken under this section is to be given in proceedings before any court or tribunal in such manner as may be provided by rules.

(3) In this section "rules" means rules of court or, in the case of proceedings before a tribunal, rules made for the purposes of this section-

(a) by the Lord Chancellor or the Secretary of State, in relation to any proceedings outside Scotland;

(b) by the Secretary of State, in relation to proceedings in Scotland; or

(c) by a Northern Ireland department, in relation to proceedings before a tribunal in Northern Ireland-

(i) which deals with transferred matters; and

(ii) for which no rules made under paragraph (a) are in force.

Subsections (2) and (3)
Provide for the procedural mechanism for giving evidence of the judgements and decisions referred to in subsection (1). This is to be done in accordance with the rules of court or, in the case of tribunals, in accordance with rules made by the Minister specified in subsection (3). Section 20 provides that rules are to be made by way of statutory instrument.

Legislation

3.– (1) So far as it is possible to do so, primary legislation and subordinate legislation must be read and given effect in a way which is compatible with the Convention rights.

Section 3
This section imposes a requirement that all legislation must be read and given effect in a way which is compatible with Convention rights, so far as it is possible to do so. This goes far beyond the previous rule that the Convention was only to be taken into account when resolving any ambiguity in domestic legislation. The practical effect is that judges will not necessarily be bound by previous interpretations of existing legislation, where such interpretations did not take account of Convention rights.

Subsection (1)
Primary and subordinate legislation are terms which are defined in section 21. The obligation to interpret legislation in a way which is compatible with Convention rights is not limited to proceedings brought under the Act but applies whenever Convention rights are relevant to an issue of interpretation of domestic legislation.

(2) This section-

    (a) applies to primary legislation and subordinate legislation whenever enacted;
    (b) does not affect the validity, continuing operation or enforcement of any incompatible primary legislation; and
    (c) does not affect the validity, continuing operation or enforcement of any incompatible subordinate legislation if (disregarding any possibility of revocation) primary legislation prevents removal of the incompatibility.

Subsection (2)
Section 3 applies to all legislation, regardless of when it was enacted. This means that legislation which was enacted prior to the Act coming into force will nevertheless be subject to the provisions of section 3. Where legislation cannot be interpreted in a manner which is compatible with Convention rights, the courts have no power to strike such legislation down. It remains in full force and effect until a declaration of incompatibility is made under section 4 and a remedial order is made under section 10. However, the courts do have the power to strike down incompatible subordinate legislation, where such action is not prevented by the relevant primary legislation.

4.– (1) Subsection (2) applies in any proceedings in which a court determines whether a provision of primary legislation is compatible with a Convention right.

(2) If the court is satisfied that the provision is incompatible with a Convention right, it may make a declaration of that incompatibility.

Section 4
This section provides that certain superior courts may make a "declaration of incompatibility" where it is found that a provision of domestic law is incompatible with a Convention right. The power to make such a declaration is discretionary and the sovereignty of Parliament is preserved, as the courts do not have the power to set aside or change such incompatible legislation.

Subsections (1) and (2)
The court may make a declaration of incompatibility in respect of primary legislation which is incompatible with a Convention right. Such a declaration can only be made in the course of proceedings in which the court determines whether a provision is compatible. There is no right to institute proceedings solely for the purpose of obtaining such a declaration.

(3) Subsection (4) applies in any proceedings in which a court determines whether a provision of subordinate legislation, made in the exercise of a power conferred by primary legislation, is compatible with a Convention right.

(4) If the court is satisfied-

 (a) that the provision is incompatible with a Convention right, and
 (b) that (disregarding any possibility of revocation) the primary legislation concerned prevents removal of the incompatibility,
it may make a declaration of that incompatibility.

> **Subsections (3) and (4)**
> *The power to make a declaration of incompatibility also extends to subordinate legislation which is incompatible with a Convention right, where the primary legislation concerned prevents the courts from removing the incompatibility.*

(5) In this section "court" means-

- (a) the House of Lords;
- (b) the Judicial Committee of the Privy Council;
- (c) the Courts-Martial Appeal Court;
- (d) in Scotland, the High Court of Justiciary sitting otherwise than as a trial court or the Court of Session;
- (e) in England and Wales or Northern Ireland, the High Court or the Court of Appeal.

> **Subsection (5)**
> *Defines the UK courts which have the power to make a declaration of incompatibility. As the power to make such a declaration is of considerable constitutional importance, it is limited to the higher courts.*

(6) A declaration under this section ("a declaration of incompatibility")-

- (a) does not affect the validity, continuing operation or enforcement of the provision in respect of which it is given; and
- (b) is not binding on the parties to the proceedings in which it is made.

> **Subsection (6)**
> *A declaration of incompatibility does not have the effect of striking down the incompatible legislation. Such legislation continues in full force and effect until Parliament makes a remedial order, in accordance with section 10 and Schedule 2. Such a declaration does not bind the parties to the proceedings in which the declaration is made.*

5.– (1) Where a court is considering whether to make a declaration of incompatibility, the Crown is entitled to notice in accordance with rules of court.

Section 5
This section places an obligation on any court which is considering whether to make a declaration of incompatibility to put the Crown on notice. This gives the Crown the opportunity to apply to be joined as a party to the proceedings and make representations to the court before the declaration is made.

subsection (1)
Where a court is considering making a declaration of incompatibility, the court must notify the Crown in accordance with the rules of court.

(2) In any case to which subsection (1) applies-

    (a) a Minister of the Crown (or a person nominated by him),
    (b) a member of the Scottish Executive,
    (c) a Northern Ireland Minister,
    (d) a Northern Ireland department,

is entitled, on giving notice in accordance with rules of court, to be joined as a party to the proceedings.

(3) Notice under subsection (2) may be given at any time during the proceedings.

subsections (2) and (3)
The persons specified in subsection (2) are entitled to apply to be joined as a party to the proceedings at any time during the proceedings in accordance with the rules of court. This enables the Crown to make representations at whatever stage in the proceedings it considers appropriate.

(4) A person who has been made a party to criminal proceedings (other than in Scotland) as the result of a notice under subsection (2) may, with leave, appeal to the House of Lords against any declaration of incompatibility made in the proceedings.

Subsection (4)
Where a person is made a party to criminal proceedings he may, with leave, appeal to the House of Lords in respect of a declaration of incompatibility. This subsection does not apply to Scotland, where the High Court of Justiciary is the final appeal court in criminal proceedings. The provision is limited to criminal proceedings because in civil proceedings any party which is joined as a party to the proceedings automatically has the same rights of appeal as the original parties.

(5) In subsection (4)-

"criminal proceedings" includes all proceedings before the Courts-Martial Appeal Court; and

"leave" means leave granted by the court making the declaration of incompatibility or by the House of Lords.

Subsection (5)
is self explanatory.

Public authorities

6.– (1) It is unlawful for a public authority to act in a way which is incompatible with a Convention right.

Section 6
This section is one of the cornerstones of the Act and provides that it is unlawful for a public authority to act in a way which is incompatible with a Convention right. This will not expose public authorities to criminal prosecution but will make them liable to the remedies which are available to the courts, as provided for in section 8.

Subsection (1)
"Public authority" is defined in subsection (3).

(2) Subsection (1) does not apply to an act if-

(a) as the result of one or more provisions of primary legislation, the authority could not have acted differently; or

(b) in the case of one or more provisions of, or made under, primary legislation which cannot be read or given effect in a way which is compatible with the Convention rights, the authority was acting so as to give effect to or enforce those provisions.

Subsection 2
An act of a public authority is not unlawful where, as a result of primary legislation, it could not have acted differently. It is also not unlawful where the authority was acting to give effect to or enforce provisions of incompatible primary legislation or subordinate legislation made under such primary legislation.

(3) In this section "public authority" includes-

(a) a court or tribunal, and
(b) any person certain of whose functions are functions of a public nature,

but does not include either House of Parliament or a person exercising functions in connection with proceedings in Parliament.

(4) In subsection (3) "Parliament" does not include the House of Lords in its judicial capacity.

Subsections (3) and (4)
Provide a wide definition of public authority. As well as including courts and tribunals (as defined in section 21), the definition will include an extensive range of bodies, such as central and local government, police, prison and immigration authorities and the BBC. It may also extend to companies such as independent television companies and the privatised utilities. It will be a matter for the courts to determine which organisations fall within the definition. Parliament is specifically excluded from the definition, apart from the House of Lords when it is sitting as a court.

(5) In relation to a particular act, a person is not a public authority by virtue only of subsection (3)(b) if the nature of the act is private.

Subsection (5)
A person is not a public authority where the nature of the act in question is private. This will affect bodies such as the privatised utilities, which perform some public and some private functions. Where such privatised utilities perform functions of a public nature, then the provisions of the Act will apply to such acts.

(6) "An act" includes a failure to act but does not include a failure to-

(a) introduce in, or lay before, Parliament a proposal for legislation; or
(b) make any primary legislation or remedial order.

Subsection (6)
An "act" includes both acts and omissions. However, it specifically excludes a failure to introduce legislation, make primary legislation or remedial orders. This prevents actions against the government for failure to legislate.

7.– (1) A person who claims that a public authority has acted (or proposes to act) in a way which is made unlawful by section 6(1) may-

    (a) bring proceedings against the authority under this Act in the appropriate court or tribunal, or

    (b) rely on the Convention right or rights concerned in any legal proceedings,

but only if he is (or would be) a victim of the unlawful act.

Section 7
This section provides that a person who is a "victim" of an unlawful act of a public authority can either bring proceedings under the Act or rely on Convention rights in any other legal proceedings.

Subsection 1
Where a person claims that a public authority has acted or proposes to act in a way which is incompatible with a Convention right, such a person may bring proceedings against the authority in the appropriate court or tribunal or rely on the Convention rights in any other legal proceedings. "Person" is not defined in the Act but includes both individuals and bodies of persons, whether corporate or unincorporate. Only persons who are actual or potential "victims", as defined in subsection (7), are entitled to bring such actions.

This section only applies where the unlawful act complained of takes place after the date when section 7 comes into force. However, where proceedings are instigated by a public authority, Convention rights can be relied upon regardless of when the unlawful act took place (section 22 (4)).

A person who brings proceedings or relies on Convention rights under section 7 is not precluded from pursuing any other remedy which is available at law (see section 11).

(2) In subsection (1)(a) "appropriate court or tribunal" means such court or tribunal as may be determined in accordance with rules; and proceedings against an authority include a counterclaim or similar proceeding.

Subsection 2
Rules, as defined in subsection (9), will be enacted which will set out which court or tribunal is appropriate for such proceedings. Proceedings under the Act can be brought by way of counter claim.

(3) If the proceedings are brought on an application for judicial review, the applicant is to be taken to have a sufficient interest in relation to the unlawful act only if he is, or would be, a victim of that act.

(4) If the proceedings are made by way of a petition for judicial review in Scotland, the applicant shall be taken to have title and interest to sue in relation to the unlawful act only if he is, or would be, a victim of that act.

Subsections (3) and (4)

It is a requirement of judicial review proceedings that the applicant satisfy the court that he has "sufficient interest".[7] This is a flexible test, allowing the courts a wide measure of discretion. The effect of this subsection is to narrow the sufficient interest test so that only persons who are victims can bring judicial review proceedings against public authorities in respect of Convention rights.

---

[7] *RSC Ord 53 r.3(7)*

---

(5) Proceedings under subsection (1)(a) must be brought before the end of-

    (a) the period of one year beginning with the date on which the act complained of took place; or

    (b) such longer period as the court or tribunal considers equitable having regard to all the circumstances,

but that is subject to any rule imposing a stricter time limit in relation to the procedure in question.

Subsection (5)

Proceedings brought against public authorities under the Act must be brought within one year of the unlawful act occurring, or within such other time limit as the court or tribunal considers equitable in all the circumstances. However, this time limit is subject to any other rules which impose a stricter time limit. For example, judicial review proceedings must be brought within 3 months from the date when the event in question arose. The time limit of one year does not apply where Convention rights are relied upon in other legal proceedings, as defined in subsection (6).

---

(6) In subsection (1)(b) "legal proceedings" includes-

    (a) proceedings brought by or at the instigation of a public authority; and

    (b) an appeal against the decision of a court or tribunal.

> **Subsection (6)**
> *Legal proceedings in which Convention rights can be relied upon include proceedings which have been instigated by public authorities and appeal proceedings.*

(7) For the purposes of this section, a person is a victim of an unlawful act only if he would be a victim for the purposes of Article 34 of the Convention if proceedings were brought in the European Court of Human Rights in respect of that act.

> **Subsection (7)**
> *This subsection has the effect of bringing to the consideration of the UK courts the large body of Convention law on the definition of "victim". Article 34 of the Convention provides that applications can be received by the Court of Human Rights from "any person, non-government organisation or group of individuals claiming to be a victim of a violation". A victim must be actually and directly affected by the unlawful act. This includes potential victims and close relatives of victims. Examples of persons who have been found by the Court of Human Rights not to be victims are pressure groups such as Greenpeace[8] and the residents of Tahiti in respect of nuclear testing on a site over 1000 kilometres away[9].*
>
> ---
>
> [8] *Greenpeace Schweiz v Switzerland and Ors (1997) 23 EHHR (CD) 116*
>
> [9] *Tauira and Ors v France (1995) D and R 83-A, 113*

(8) Nothing in this Act creates a criminal offence.

> **Subsection (8)**
> *Although nothing in the Act creates a criminal offence, this does not affect the fact that certain violations of Convention rights, such as unlawful imprisonment and torture, already amount to a criminal offence.*

(9) In this section "rules" means-

    (a) in relation to proceedings before a court or tribunal outside Scotland, rules made by the Lord Chancellor or the Secretary of State for the purposes of this section or rules of court,

    (b) in relation to proceedings before a court or tribunal in Scotland, rules made by the Secretary of State for those purposes,

    (c) in relation to proceedings before a tribunal in Northern Ireland-

        (i) which deals with transferred matters; and

(ii) for which no rules made under paragraph (a) are in force,

rules made by a Northern Ireland department for those purposes,

and includes provision made by order under section 1 of the Courts and Legal Services Act 1990.

Subsection (9)
This subsection defines "rules".

(10) In making rules, regard must be had to section 9.

Subsection (10)
is self explanatory

(11) The Minister who has power to make rules in relation to a particular tribunal may, to the extent he considers it necessary to ensure that the tribunal can provide an appropriate remedy in relation to an act (or proposed act) of a public authority which is (or would be) unlawful as a result of section 6(1), by order add to-

(a) the relief or remedies which the tribunal may grant; or
(b) the grounds on which it may grant any of them.

Subsection (11)
Where a particular tribunal does not have jurisdiction to hear cases which involve Convention rights, this subsection enables the Minister with power to make rules in relation to such a tribunal to give the tribunal jurisdiction to determine such cases and to grant such relief or remedy as is within its power. This must be done by order and under section 20(4) such an order cannot be made unless a draft of the order is placed before and approved by each House of Parliament.

(12) An order made under subsection (11) may contain such incidental, supplemental, consequential or transitional provision as the Minister making it considers appropriate.

(13) "The Minister" includes the Northern Ireland department concerned.

Subsections (12) and (13)
are self explanatory

8.– (1) In relation to any act (or proposed act) of a public authority which the court finds is (or would be) unlawful, it may grant such relief or remedy, or make such order, within its powers as it considers just and appropriate.

Section 8
This section makes provision for a court or tribunal to grant such relief or remedy as it considers appropriate where a public authority has acted, or proposes to act, unlawfully.

Subsection (1)
is self explanatory

(2) But damages may be awarded only by a court which has power to award damages, or to order the payment of compensation, in civil proceedings.

Subsection (2)
Criminal courts do not have the power to award damages or compensation in respect of Convention violations. Damages are restricted to civil proceedings. However, there are other remedies which it would be open to the criminal courts to grant, such as staying proceedings, quashing indictments and excluding evidence.

(3) No award of damages is to be made unless, taking account of all the circumstances of the case, including-

(a) any other relief or remedy granted, or order made, in relation to the act in question (by that or any other court), and

(b) the consequences of any decision (of that or any other court) in respect of that act,

the court is satisfied that the award is necessary to afford just satisfaction to the person in whose favour it is made.

Subsection (3)
Damages can only be awarded once the court has taken all relevant matters into consideration, including any other damages awarded in other proceedings arising from the same act. As often happens with decisions of the Court of Human Rights, a simple finding that an unlawful act has occurred may be considered a sufficient remedy in all the circumstances.

(4) In determining-

(a) whether to award damages, or
(b) the amount of an award,

the court must take into account the principles applied by the European Court of Human Rights in relation to the award of compensation under Article 41 of the Convention.

Subsection (4)
Courts must follow the principles which are applied by the Court of Human Rights when awarding damages. Article 41 of the Convention provides that an injured party should be afforded "just satisfaction". The level of damages awarded by UK courts must be commensurate with the level of damages awarded by the Court of Human Rights. Such awards usually range between £5000-£15,000. In practice, this means that awards of damages will either be non- existent or relatively low.

(5) A public authority against which damages are awarded is to be treated-

(a) in Scotland, for the purposes of section 3 of the Law Reform (Miscellaneous Provisions) (Scotland) Act 1940 as if the award were made in an action of damages in which the authority has been found liable in respect of loss or damage to the person to whom the award is made;
(b) for the purposes of the Civil Liability (Contribution) Act 1978 as liable in respect of damage suffered by the person to whom the award is made.

Subsection (5)
These statutory provisions provide for a right to contribution when more than one person is liable for the same damage and the purpose of this subsection is to make such provisions applicable when damages are awarded against a public authority under the Act.

(6) In this section-

"court" includes a tribunal;

"damages" means damages for an unlawful act of a public authority; and

"unlawful" means unlawful under section 6(1).

Subsection (6)
is self explanatory

9.– (1) Proceedings under section 7(1)(a) in respect of a judicial act may be brought only-

(a) by exercising a right of appeal;
(b) on an application (in Scotland a petition) for judicial review; or
(c) in such other forum as may be prescribed by rules.

Section 9
This section specifies the way in which judicial acts can be reviewed and preserves the rule that judges, magistrates, court clerks, tribunal members and officers of the court are immune from legal proceedings in respect of acts done in the performance of their functions.

Subsection (1)
Where a court or tribunal acts in a way which is incompatible with a Convention right, an aggrieved party's remedy is restricted to exercising his right to appeal, applying for judicial review, (where such an application is permitted at law), or following such other procedure which is laid down in rules, as defined in section 7 (9).

(2) That does not affect any rule of law which prevents a court from being the subject of judicial review.

Subsection (2)
Acts of inferior courts can be the subject of judicial review proceedings but acts of superior courts cannot be judicially reviewed.

(3) In proceedings under this Act in respect of a judicial act done in good faith, damages may not be awarded otherwise than to compensate a person to the extent required by Article 5(5) of the Convention.

Subsection (3)
Unless bad faith can be established, damages cannot be awarded against the Crown in respect of judicial acts. The sole exception is compensation which may be awarded under Article 5 (5) of the Convention, which relates to persons who are arrested or detained unlawfully.

(4) An award of damages permitted by subsection (3) is to be made against the Crown; but no award may be made unless the appropriate person, if not a party to the proceedings, is joined.

Subsection (4)
If damages are awarded for judicial acts, the award is against the Crown and not against the judge involved. The Minister responsible for the court or tribunal concerned, or his nominee, must be joined as a party before an award of damages can be made.

(5) In this section-

"appropriate person" means the Minister responsible for the court concerned, or a person or government department nominated by him;

"court" includes a tribunal;

"judge" includes a member of a tribunal, a justice of the peace and a clerk or other officer entitled to exercise the jurisdiction of a court;

"judicial act" means a judicial act of a court and includes an act done on the instructions, or on behalf, of a judge; and

"rules" has the same meaning as in section 7(9).

Subsection (5)
is self explanatory.

Remedial action

10.– (1) This section applies if-

   (a) a provision of legislation has been declared under section 4 to be incompatible with a Convention right and, if an appeal lies-

     (i) all persons who may appeal have stated in writing that they do not intend to do so;

     (ii) the time for bringing an appeal has expired and no appeal has been brought within that time; or

     (iii) an appeal brought within that time has been determined or abandoned; or

   (b) it appears to a Minister of the Crown or Her Majesty in Council that, having regard to a finding of the European Court of Human Rights made after the coming into force of this section in proceedings against the United Kingdom, a provision of legislation is incompatible with an obligation of the United Kingdom arising from the Convention.

Section 10

This section makes provision for legislation which is incompatible with Convention rights to be remedied by Parliament.

Subsection (1)

Action to remedy incompatible legislation may be taken by the relevant Minister where a declaration of incompatibility has been made under section 4 and the appeal process is complete. It can also be taken when there has been a decision of the Court of Human Rights and as a result of such a decision the Minister is of the view that certain legislation is incompatible. Only decisions of the Court of Human Rights made after section 10 comes into force can trigger such remedial action.

(2) If a Minister of the Crown considers that there are compelling reasons for proceeding under this section, he may by order make such amendments to the legislation as he considers necessary to remove the incompatibility.

Subsection (2)

The power to take remedial action is discretionary and can only be exercised where a Minister decides that there are "compelling reasons" to do so. If remedial action is required, the Minister will make a remedial order to amend or repeal the incompatible legislation. Such orders must be approved by a resolution of each House of Parliament. The detailed procedures for making such orders are set out in Schedule 2.

(3) If, in the case of subordinate legislation, a Minister of the Crown considers-

    (a) that it is necessary to amend the primary legislation under which the subordinate legislation in question was made, in order to enable the incompatibility to be removed, and

    (b) that there are compelling reasons for proceeding under this section,

he may by order make such amendments to the primary legislation as he considers necessary.

Subsection (3)
The power to make remedial orders also applies where it is necessary to remove an incompatibility in subordinate legislation by amending the primary legislation under which such incompatible subordinate legislation was made. Again, there must be compelling reasons to do so and the procedures set out in Schedule 2 must be followed.

(4) This section also applies where the provision in question is in subordinate legislation and has been quashed, or declared invalid, by reason of incompatibility with a Convention right and the Minister proposes to proceed under paragraph 2(b) of Schedule 2.

Subsection (4)
Remedial orders may also be made where subordinate legislation has been quashed or declared invalid by the higher courts because it is incompatible with Convention rights. The higher courts do have the power to act in such a way where the primary legislation under which such incompatible subordinate legislation was put in place does not prevent such action.

(5) If the legislation is an Order in Council, the power conferred by subsection (2) or (3) is exercisable by Her Majesty in Council.

Subsection (5)
An Order in Council is made by the Queen by and with the advice of the Privy Council. Accordingly, any remedial orders in respect of such Orders must be made by Her Majesty in Council.

(6) In this section "legislation" does not include a Measure of the Church Assembly or of the General Synod of the Church of England.

Subsection (6)
is self explanatory

(7) Schedule 2 makes further provision about remedial orders.

Subsection (7)
Schedule 2 contains the detailed procedures which must be followed when making a remedial order.

Other rights and proceedings

11. A person's reliance on a Convention right does not restrict-

  (a) any other right or freedom conferred on him by or under any law having effect in any part of the United Kingdom; or
  (b) his right to make any claim or bring any proceedings which he could make or bring apart from sections 7 to 9.

Section 11
This section gives effect to Article 53 of the Convention and provides that where a person relies on a Convention right or brings proceedings under the Act this does not prevent him from relying on any other rights or freedoms which he enjoys at law or from bringing any other proceedings available at law.

12.– (1) This section applies if a court is considering whether to grant any relief which, if granted, might affect the exercise of the Convention right to freedom of expression.

Section 12
The purpose of this section is to safeguard the freedom of the press and to ensure that courts have particular regard to Article 10 of the Convention, which relates to freedom of expression, when considering the grant of any relief which might affect such freedom. This section will mainly affect injunctions.

Subsection (1)
This is widely drafted so that section 12 applies wherever a court is considering granting any relief which might affect the freedom of expression. "Relief" is defined in subsection (5). This section is not limited to cases where a public authority is a party but applies to any person whose right to freedom of expression may be affected by the relief which is sought.

(2) If the person against whom the application for relief is made ("the respondent") is neither present nor represented, no such relief is to be granted unless the court is satisfied-

   (a) that the applicant has taken all practicable steps to notify the respondent; or
   (b) that there are compelling reasons why the respondent should not be notified.

Subsection (2)
Where the person against whom the application for relief is made is not present or represented at the hearing, the court must not grant the relief unless it is satisfied that all practicable steps have been taken to notify the other party or that there are compelling reasons why the other party should not be notified. Compelling reasons would be matters such as national security.

(3) No such relief is to be granted so as to restrain publication before trial unless the court is satisfied that the applicant is likely to establish that publication should not be allowed.

Subsection (3)
Courts cannot grant relief to restrain publication before trial unless satisfied that the party seeking such relief would be likely to establish at trial that publication should not be allowed.

(4) The court must have particular regard to the importance of the Convention right to freedom of expression and, where the proceedings relate to material which the respondent claims, or which appears to the court, to be journalistic, literary or artistic material (or to conduct connected with such material), to-

  (a) the extent to which-
      (i) the material has, or is about to, become available to the public; or
      (ii) it is, or would be, in the public interest for the material to be published;
  (b) any relevant privacy code.

Subsection (4)
Courts must have particular regard to Article 10 and its associated jurisprudence. In practice, the decisions of the Court of Human Rights have generally upheld the freedom of the press. In respect of journalistic, literary or artistic material, the courts must have particular regard to the extent to which such material is, or is about to be available to the public and whether it is in the public interest for such material to be published. "Public" is not defined or qualified in any way and it will be a matter for the courts to interpret the term. Particular regard must also be given to any relevant privacy code, such as the Press Complaints Commission and Independent Television Commission Code.

(5) In this section-

  "court" includes a tribunal; and

  "relief" includes any remedy or order (other than in criminal proceedings).

Subsection (5)
Defines "relief" in wide terms and provides that section 12 does not apply to criminal proceedings.

13.– (1) If a court's determination of any question arising under this Act might affect the exercise by a religious organisation (itself or its members collectively) of the Convention right to freedom of thought, conscience and religion, it must have particular regard to the importance of that right.

(2) In this section

  "court" includes a tribunal.

Section 13

The effect of the Act on the church and other religious organisations was a matter of great concern and was extensively debated in Parliament. This section was introduced by the Government to ensure that those concerns were met. It provides that the courts must have particular regard to the right of freedom of thought, conscience and religion guaranteed by Article 9 of the Convention when considering any question under the Act which might affect such a right.

Subsection (1)

Most of the actions of a religious organisation are, in general, private in nature and would not therefore be open to challenge under the provisions of the Act (see section 6(5)). However, where religious organisations carry out functions of a public nature, such as performing marriage ceremonies or running church schools, the Act will apply, as the religious organisation would be a "public authority".

Where an act of a religious organisation is challenged under the Act, the courts must have particular regard to Article 9 and to the jurisprudence of Convention institutions, which have generally upheld the right of religious organisations to practice their genuinely held beliefs. The term "religious organisation" has not been defined, as there is no definition readily available in UK or Strasbourg jurisprudence. Which organisations fall within the definition will be a matter for the courts to decide but it will be flexible enough to cover such organisations as religious charities.

Subsection (2)

is self explanatory.

Derogations and reservations

14.– (1) In this Act "designated derogation" means-

    (a) the United Kingdom's derogation from Article 5(3) of the Convention; and

    (b) any derogation by the United Kingdom from an Article of the Convention, or of any protocol to the Convention, which is designated for the purposes of this Act in an order made by the Secretary of State.

(2) The derogation referred to in subsection (1)(a) is set out in Part I of Schedule 3.

Section 14

The Convention rights which are given effect to in section 1 are subject to any designated derogation. This section defines the term "designated derogation" and makes provision in respect of such designated derogations.

Subsections (1) and (2)
Designated derogation is defined as the derogation set out in Part 1 of Schedule 3 and any other derogation designated by order of the Secretary of State.

(3) If a designated derogation is amended or replaced it ceases to be a designated derogation.

(4) But subsection (3) does not prevent the Secretary of State from exercising his power under subsection (1)(b) to make a fresh designation order in respect of the Article concerned.

Subsections (3) and (4)
If a designated derogation is amended or replaced it ceases to be a designated derogation, although the Secretary of State can make a fresh designation order in respect of the Convention Article in question.

(5) The Secretary of State must by order make such amendments to Schedule 3 as he considers appropriate to reflect-

   (a) any designation order; or
   (b) the effect of subsection (3).

Subsection (5)
Requires the Secretary of State to amend Schedule 3 as necessary to reflect any changes.

(6) A designation order may be made in anticipation of the making by the United Kingdom of a proposed derogation.

subsection (6)
is self explanatory

15.– (1) In this Act "designated reservation" means-

   (a) the United Kingdom's reservation to Article 2 of the First Protocol to the Convention; and

(b) any other reservation by the United Kingdom to an Article of the Convention, or of any protocol to the Convention, which is designated for the purposes of this Act in an order made by the Secretary of State.

(2) The text of the reservation referred to in subsection (1)(a) is set out in Part II of Schedule 3.

Section 15
The Convention rights which are given effect to in section 1 are also subject to any designated reservation, which is defined in this section.

Subsections 1 and 2
These subsections define "designated reservation" as that set out in Part II of Schedule 3, together with any other reservation designated in an order by the Secretary of State.

(3) If a designated reservation is withdrawn wholly or in part it ceases to be a designated reservation.

Subsection 3
As it is not possible for a state to amend or replace a reservation once the Protocol in question has been ratified, where a reservation is withdrawn wholly or in part it ceases to be a designated reservation.

(4) But subsection (3) does not prevent the Secretary of State from exercising his power under subsection (1)(b) to make a fresh designation order in respect of the Article concerned.

Subsection 4
This provides that the Secretary of State has the power by order to make a fresh designation order.

(5) The Secretary of State must by order make such amendments to this Act as he considers appropriate to reflect-

(a) any designation order; or
(b) the effect of subsection (3).

> **Subsection 5**
> *This requires the Secretary of State to amend the Act by order where necessary in order to reflect any changes.*

16.– (1) If it has not already been withdrawn by the United Kingdom, a designated derogation ceases to have effect for the purposes of this Act-

    (a) in the case of the derogation referred to in section 14(1)(a), at the end of the period of five years beginning with the date on which section 1(2) came into force;

    (b) in the case of any other derogation, at the end of the period of five years beginning with the date on which the order designating it was made.

> **Section 16**
> *As derogations apply only in situations of war or public emergency, they are by nature limited in time. This section provides that derogations shall last for a period of five years, unless extended by order.*
>
> **Subsection (1)**
> *Unless earlier withdrawn, the existing derogation specified in Schedule 3 shall cease to have effect 5 years after the entry into force of section 1 (2). Any other derogations shall cease to have effect 5 years after the date of the order designating that it be made.*

(2) At any time before the period-

    (a) fixed by subsection (1)(a) or (b), or

    (b) extended by an order under this subsection,

comes to an end, the Secretary of State may by order extend it by a further period of five years.

> **Subsection (2)**
> *Allows the Secretary of State, by order, to extend derogations for a further period of five years and thereafter for successive periods of five years. Under section 20, a draft of such an order must be laid before both Houses of Parliament.*

(3) An order under section 14(1)(b) ceases to have effect at the end of the period for consideration, unless a resolution has been passed by each House approving the order.

(4) Subsection (3) does not affect-

    (a) anything done in reliance on the order; or
    (b) the power to make a fresh order under section 14(1)(b).

(5) In subsection (3) "period for consideration" means the period of forty days beginning with the day on which the order was made.

(6) In calculating the period for consideration, no account is to be taken of any time during which-

    (a) Parliament is dissolved or prorogued; or
    (b) both Houses are adjourned for more than four days.

Subsections (3)-(6)
An order made under section 14(1)(b) which designates a derogation takes immediate effect. However, such an order will cease to have effect unless it is approved by both Houses of Parliament within 40 days. If Parliament does not approve the order, this will not affect anything done during the 40 day period in reliance on the order nor will it prevent the Secretary of State from making a fresh order. The periods mentioned in subsection (6) are not counted when calculating the 40 day period.

(7) If a designated derogation is withdrawn by the United Kingdom, the Secretary of State must by order make such amendments to this Act as he considers are required to reflect that withdrawal.

Subsection (7)
Appropriate amendments to the Act must be made by the Secretary of State if a designated derogation is withdrawn.

17.– (1) The appropriate Minister must review the designated reservation referred to in section 15(1)(a)-

    (a) before the end of the period of five years beginning with the date on which section 1(2) came into force; and

(b) if that designation is still in force, before the end of the period of five years beginning with the date on which the last report relating to it was laid under subsection (3).

> **Section 17**
> *This section provides that reservations must be periodically reviewed by the appropriate Minister, as defined in section 21.*
>
> **Subsection (1)**
> *The UK's existing reservation set out in Schedule 3 must be reviewed by the appropriate Minister within 5 years of the date when section 1(2) of the Act enters into force and every five years thereafter.*

(2) The appropriate Minister must review each of the other designated reservations (if any)-

(a) before the end of the period of five years beginning with the date on which the order designating the reservation first came into force; and

(b) if the designation is still in force, before the end of the period of five years beginning with the date on which the last report relating to it was laid under subsection (3).

> **Subsection (2)**
> *Any other designated reservation must be reviewed within five years of the date when the order creating it came into force and every five years thereafter.*

(3) The Minister conducting a review under this section must prepare a report on the result of the review and lay a copy of it before each House of Parliament.

> **Subsection (3)**
> *is self explanatory.*

Judges of the European Court of Human Rights

18.– (1) In this section "judicial office" means the office of-

(a) Lord Justice of Appeal, Justice of the High Court or Circuit judge, in England and Wales;

(b) judge of the Court of Session or sheriff, in Scotland;

(c) Lord Justice of Appeal, judge of the High Court or county court judge, in Northern Ireland.

Section 18

Since the entry into force of the Eleventh Protocol, the Court of Human Rights is now a full time court. This section makes provision for the appointment of UK judges to the Court of Human Rights.

Subsection (1)

This subsection specifies which level of UK judge is eligible for appointment to the Court of Human Rights.

---

(2) The holder of a judicial office may become a judge of the European Court of Human Rights ("the Court") without being required to relinquish his office.

(3) But he is not required to perform the duties of his judicial office while he is a judge of the Court.

Subsections (2) and (3)

It is possible for a UK judge to become a judge in the Court of Human Rights without having to resign from his appointment in the UK or to continue to perform any of his duties in the UK during his appointment to the Court of Human Rights.

---

(4) In respect of any period during which he is a judge of the Court-

(a) a Lord Justice of Appeal or Justice of the High Court is not to count as a judge of the relevant court for the purposes of section 2(1) or 4(1) of the Supreme Court Act 1981 (maximum number of judges) nor as a judge of the Supreme Court for the purposes of section 12(1) to (6) of that Act (salaries etc.);

(b) a judge of the Court of Session is not to count as a judge of that court for the purposes of section 1(1) of the Court of Session Act 1988 (maximum number of judges) or of section 9(1)(c) of the Administration of Justice Act 1973 ("the 1973 Act") (salaries etc.);

(c) a Lord Justice of Appeal or judge of the High Court in Northern Ireland is not to count as a judge of the relevant court for the purposes of section 2(1) or 3(1) of the Judicature (Northern Ireland) Act 1978 (maximum number of judges) nor as a judge of the Supreme Court of Northern Ireland for the purposes of section 9(1)(d) of the 1973 Act (salaries etc.);

(d) a Circuit judge is not to count as such for the purposes of section 18 of the Courts Act 1971 (salaries etc.);

(e) a sheriff is not to count as such for the purposes of section 14 of the Sheriff Courts (Scotland) Act 1907 (salaries etc.);

(f) a county court judge of Northern Ireland is not to count as such for the purposes of section 106 of the County Courts Act Northern Ireland) 1959 (salaries etc.).

Subsection (4)
UK judges who become judges of the Court of Human Rights will be paid by the Council of Europe during their tenure and will not be entitled to their UK judicial salary. Where there is a statutory limit on the number of judges in any of the UK offices, UK judges who are appointed to the Court of Human Rights will not be counted for the purposes of such a limit.

(5) If a sheriff principal is appointed a judge of the Court, section 11(1) of the Sheriff Courts (Scotland) Act 1971 (temporary appointment of sheriff principal) applies, while he holds that appointment, as if his office is vacant.

Subsection (5)
Where necessary, temporary sheriff principals may to be appointed in Scotland.

(6) Schedule 4 makes provision about judicial pensions in relation to the holder of a judicial office who serves as a judge of the Court.

Subsection (6)
Schedule 4 makes provision for judicial pensions and ensures that a UK judge's pension will not be prejudiced by an appointment to the Court of Human Rights.

(7) The Lord Chancellor or the Secretary of State may by order make such transitional provision (including, in particular, provision for a temporary increase in the maximum number of judges) as he considers appropriate in relation to any holder of a judicial office who has completed his service as a judge of the Court.

> **Subsection (7)**
> *allows a degree of flexibility to make such orders as are appropriate when a judge returns to the UK after serving in Strasbourg.*

Parliamentary procedure

19.– (1) A Minister of the Crown in charge of a Bill in either House of Parliament must, before Second Reading of the Bill-

(a) make a statement to the effect that in his view the provisions of the Bill are compatible with the Convention rights ("a statement of compatibility"); or

(b) make a statement to the effect that although he is unable to make a statement of compatibility the government nevertheless wishes the House to proceed with the Bill.

> **Section 19**
> *Makes provision for "statements of compatibility' in respect of all new legislation proceeding through Parliament.*
>
> **Subsection (1)**
> *In respect of all new legislation, prior to the Second Reading of the Bill the Minister responsible must either make a statement that such legislation is compatible with Convention rights or make a statement that such a statement cannot be made but the Government nevertheless wishes the Bill to proceed. This ensures that the issue of whether a new piece of legislation is compatible with Convention rights is addressed at an early stage in the Parliamentary procedure and fully debated where necessary.*

(2) The statement must be in writing and be published in such manner as the Minister making it considers appropriate.

> **Subsection (2)**
> *is self explanatory.*

Supplemental

20.– (1) Any power of a Minister of the Crown to make an order under this Act is exercisable by statutory instrument.

(2) The power of the Lord Chancellor or the Secretary of State to make rules (other than rules of court) under section 2(3) or 7(9) is exercisable by statutory instrument.

(3) Any statutory instrument made under section 14, 15 or 16(7) must be laid before Parliament.

(4) No order may be made by the Lord Chancellor or the Secretary of State under section 1(4), 7(11) or 16(2) unless a draft of the order has been laid before, and approved by, each House of Parliament.

(5) Any statutory instrument made under section 18(7) or Schedule 4, or to which subsection (2) applies, shall be subject to annulment in pursuance of a resolution of either House of Parliament.

(6) The power of a Northern Ireland department to make-

(a) rules under section 2(3)(c) or 7(9)(c), or
(b) an order under section 7(11),

is exercisable by statutory rule for the purposes of the Statutory Rules (Northern Ireland) Order 1979.

(7) Any rules made under section 2(3)(c) or 7(9)(c) shall be subject to negative resolution; and section 41(6) of the Interpretation Act (Northern Ireland) 1954 (meaning of "subject to negative resolution") shall apply as if the power to make the rules were conferred by an Act of the Northern Ireland Assembly.

(8) No order may be made by a Northern Ireland department under section 7(11) unless a draft of the order has been laid before, and approved by, the Northern Ireland Assembly.

Section 20
This section contains specific technical provisions for the way in which rules and orders are to be made under the Act.

21.– (1) In this Act-

"amend" includes repeal and apply (with or without modifications);

"the appropriate Minister" means the Minister of the Crown having charge of the appropriate authorised government department (within the meaning of the Crown Proceedings Act 1947);

"the Commission" means the European Commission of Human Rights;

"the Convention" means the Convention for the Protection of Human Rights and Fundamental Freedoms, agreed by the Council of Europe at Rome on 4th

November 1950 as it has effect for the time being in relation to the United Kingdom;

"declaration of incompatibility" means a declaration under section 4;

"Minister of the Crown" has the same meaning as in the Ministers of the Crown Act 1975;

"Northern Ireland Minister" includes the First Minister and the deputy First Minister in Northern Ireland;

"primary legislation" means any-

(a) public general Act;
(b) local and personal Act;
(c) private Act;
(d) Measure of the Church Assembly;
(e) Measure of the General Synod of the Church of England;
(f) Order in Council-
   (i) made in exercise of Her Majesty's Royal Prerogative;
   (ii) made under section 38(1)(a) of the Northern Ireland Constitution Act 1973 or the corresponding provision of the Northern Ireland Act 1998; or
   (iii) amending an Act of a kind mentioned in paragraph (a), (b) or (c);

and includes an order or other instrument made under primary legislation (otherwise than by the National Assembly for Wales, a member of the Scottish Executive, a Northern Ireland Minister or a Northern Ireland department) to the extent to which it operates to bring one or more provisions of that legislation into force or amends any primary legislation;

"the First Protocol" means the protocol to the Convention agreed at Paris on 20th March 1952;

"the Sixth Protocol" means the protocol to the Convention agreed at Strasbourg on 28th April 1983;

"the Eleventh Protocol" means the protocol to the Convention (restructuring the control machinery established by the Convention) agreed at Strasbourg on 11th May 1994;

"remedial order" means an order under section 10;

"subordinate legislation" means any-

(a) Order in Council other than one-
   (i) made in exercise of Her Majesty's Royal Prerogative;
   (ii) made under section 38(1)(a) of the Northern Ireland Constitution Act 1973 or the corresponding provision of the Northern Ireland Act 1998; or
   (iii) amending an Act of a kind mentioned in the definition of primary legislation;

(b) Act of the Scottish Parliament;

(c) Act of the Parliament of Northern Ireland;

(d) Measure of the Assembly established under section 1 of the Northern Ireland Assembly Act 1973;

(e) Act of the Northern Ireland Assembly;

(f) order, rules, regulations, scheme, warrant, byelaw or other instrument made under primary legislation (except to the extent to which it operates to bring one or more provisions of that legislation into force or amends any primary legislation);

(g) order, rules, regulations, scheme, warrant, byelaw or other instrument made under legislation mentioned in paragraph (b), (c), (d) or (e) or made under an Order in Council applying only to Northern Ireland;

(h) order, rules, regulations, scheme, warrant, byelaw or other instrument made by a member of the Scottish Executive, a Northern Ireland Minister or a Northern Ireland department in exercise of prerogative or other executive functions of Her Majesty which are exercisable by such a person on behalf of Her Majesty;

"transferred matters" has the same meaning as in the Northern Ireland Act 1998; and

"tribunal" means any tribunal in which legal proceedings may be brought.

Section 21
This section contains a number of important definitions and other provisions concerning interpretation.

Subsection (1)
is self explanatory.

(2) The references in paragraphs (b) and (c) of section 2(1) to Articles are to Articles of the Convention as they had effect immediately before the coming into force of the Eleventh Protocol.

(3) The reference in paragraph (d) of section 2(1) to Article 46 includes a reference to Articles 32 and 54 of the Convention as they had effect immediately before the coming into force of the Eleventh Protocol.

Subsections (2) and (3)
The Eleventh Protocol made a significant number of procedural changes to the Convention. As a result, some Articles of the Convention have been renumbered, with effect from 1 November 1998. References in the Act to Convention Articles are to the renumbered Articles, with the exception of section 2(1) (b), (c) and (d), where the references are to Articles before they were amended by the Eleventh Protocol.

(4) The references in section 2(1) to a report or decision of the Commission or a decision of the Committee of Ministers include references to a report or decision made as provided by paragraphs 3, 4 and 6 of Article 5 of the Eleventh Protocol (transitional provisions).

Subsection (4)
There are transitional arrangements in place until such time as the new Court of Human Rights is fully established.

(5) Any liability under the Army Act 1955, the Air Force Act 1955 or the Naval Discipline Act 1957 to suffer death for an offence is replaced by a liability to imprisonment for life or any less punishment authorised by those Acts; and those Acts shall accordingly have effect with the necessary modifications.

Subsection (5)
This subsection makes the necessary amendments to legislation in respect of the Forces and reflects the inclusion in the Act of the Sixth Protocol.

22.– (1) This Act may be cited as the Human Rights Act 1998.

Section 22
This section deals with a number of miscellaneous matters.

Subsection (1)
is self explanatory.

(2) Sections 18, 20 and 21(5) and this section come into force on the passing of this Act.

(3) The other provisions of this Act come into force on such day as the Secretary of State may by order appoint; and different days may be appointed for different · purposes.

Subsections (2) and (3)
It is not expected that the main provisions of the Act will come into force before the early part of 2000.

(4) Paragraph (b) of subsection (1) of section 7 applies to proceedings brought by or at the instigation of a public authority whenever the act in question took place; but otherwise that subsection does not apply to an act taking place before the coming into force of that section.

Subsection (4)
A person cannot proceed against a public authority or rely on Convention rights in legal proceedings in respect of acts which take place prior to the date when section 7 comes into force. However, where a public authority instigates proceedings, Convention rights can be relied upon, even where the act in question takes place prior to section 7 coming into force.

(5) This Act binds the Crown.

Subsection (5)
is self explanatory.

(6) This Act extends to Northern Ireland.

Subsection (6)
The Act applies to England and Wales, Scotland and Northern Ireland.

(7) Section 21(5), so far as it relates to any provision contained in the Army Act 1955, the Air Force Act 1955 or the Naval Discipline Act 1957, extends to any place to which that provision extends.

Subsection (7)
is self explanatory.

SCHEDULES

SCHEDULE 1

THE ARTICLES

PART I

THE CONVENTION

RIGHTS AND FREEDOMS

ARTICLE 2

Right to life

1. Everyone's right to life shall be protected by law. No one shall be deprived of his life intentionally save in the execution of a sentence of a court following his conviction of a crime for which this penalty is provided by law.

ARTICLE 2 (1)

Following the horrific disrespect for human life during the Second World War, it was thought essential that the most fundamental freedom of the right to life should be protected. Therefore, the states that agreed the Convention set out to prevent the taking of life of any citizen. The only justification for depriving an individual of life would be if the state's action fell within certain exceptional circumstances.

A state cannot derogate from or reserve its position in relation to Article 2.

The principal objective of Article 2 was to prohibit the arbitrary taking of life by the state, but the Court of Human Rights has clearly extended the nature of the state's responsibility. It has been held that the term 'protected by law' places two distinct obligations upon the state. Firstly, the state itself is prevented from the intentional taking of life. Secondly, it must ensure that appropriate steps are taken to safeguard life.[10] This second obligation applies to actions by the state itself and to the actions of private individuals. Accordingly, national legislation must be implemented that protects the citizen's right to life.

In line with this requirement, the deliberate taking of another person's life is a criminal offence. The mandatory sentence imposed for murder in the UK is a term of life imprisonment.

[10] *Application 7154/75 X v UK 14 DR 31 p. 32(1978).*

2. Deprivation of life shall not be regarded as inflicted in contravention of this Article when it results from the use of force which is no more than absolutely necessary:

   (a) in defence of any person from unlawful violence;
   (b) in order to effect a lawful arrest or to prevent the escape of a person lawfully detained;
   (c) in action lawfully taken for the purpose of quelling a riot or insurrection.

These exceptional circumstances where the deprivation of life may be justified are exhaustive and must be narrowly interpreted by the courts.

'No More than Absolutely Necessary'
This term places an essential check on the permitted use of force. Such a strict condition of necessity implies that the use of force must only be used in emergency situations.

The main question will centre on whether the state's response was proportionate to the perceived threat. Essentially, if an alternative measure can be adopted, then the use of such life threatening force should not be used.[11] The Court of Human Rights has stated that:

'the use of lethal force by agents of the State in pursuit of one of the aims delineated in paragraph 2 of Article 2 of the Convention may be justified ... where it is based on an honest belief which is perceived, for good reasons, to be valid at the time... To hold otherwise would be to impose an unrealistic burden on the State and its law enforcement personnel in the execution of their duty, perhaps to the detriment of their lives and those of others.'[12]

'Lawful arrest'
'Lawful arrest' means an arrest that complies with domestic law.

---

[11] *Kelly v UK (1993) 16 EHRR CD 20*

[12] *Mc Cann and others 27th September 1995 Series A no.324 para.200.*

ARTICLE 3

Prohibition of torture

No one shall be subjected to torture or to inhuman or degrading treatment or punishment.

ARTICLE 3 - PROHIBITION OF TORTURE
There is no derogation permitted from this Article.

'Torture'
The Court of Human Rights has defined torture as:

'deliberate inhuman treatment causing very serious and cruel suffering.' [13]

The Commission have given examples of such torture and ill-treatment;

— *beating the soles of a prisoner's feet;*

— *electro-shock treatment;*

— *mock executions;*

— *threats to shoot or kill the detainee.*

'Torture' also includes treatment that is aimed at mental suffering which creates a state of anguish and stress in the detainee. Less serious cases than torture are likely to be regarded as 'inhuman or degrading treatment or punishment'.

"Inhuman treatment or punishment"
The Court of Human Rights defined this term as:

'the infliction of intense physical and mental suffering.'

The Court added:

' Ill treatment must attain a minimum level of severity if it is to fall within the scope of Article 3. The assessment of this minimum is, in the nature of things, relative; it depends on all the circumstances of the case, such as the duration of the treatment, its physical or mental effects and, in some cases, the sex, age and state of health of the victim, etc.' [14]

[13] *Ireland v UK 18th January 1978 Series A no.25 pp.66-67*

[14] *Ireland v UK (1978) as above.*

'Degrading treatment'
Defined by the Court of Human Rights as:

'ill treatment designed to arouse in victims feelings of fear, anguish and inferiority capable of humiliating and debasing them and possibly breaking their physical and moral resistance.' [15]

The Commission has further stated that "degrading" goes beyond the terms disagreeable and uncomfortable in terms of severity. [16]

Examples of violations under this Article have included ill treatment of prisoners, the deportation of refugees to countries where there is a real risk of such treatment and the use of degrading corporal punishment.

---

[15] *Ireland v UK 18th January 1978 Series A no.25 pp.66-67.*

[16] *Lopez Ostra Judgment 9th December 1994 Series A no.303-C*

ARTICLE 4

Prohibition of slavery and forced labour

1. No one shall be held in slavery or servitude.

ARTICLE 4 – PROHIBITION OF SLAVERY AND FORCED LABOUR

Article 4 (1)
No state can derogate from this fundamental freedom.

'Slavery'
'Slavery' has been defined as a "status or condition of a person over whom any or all of the powers attaching to the right of ownership are exercised." [17]

Slavery was abolished by the British Parliament in 1833.

'Servitude'
'Servitude' suggests a lesser restraint than slavery but would involve a serious form of denial of freedom.[18]

---

[17] *Slavery Convention 1926.*

[18] *Van Doogenbroeck v Belgium Series A no.50 (1982) 4 EHRR 443.*

2. No one shall be required to perform forced or compulsory labour.

Article 4 (2) -

'Forced and compulsory labour'
The Court of Human Rights has defined 'compulsory labour' as:

'all work or service which is exacted from any person under the menace of any penalty and for which the said person has not offered himself voluntarily.' [19]

If the complainant had voluntarily undertaken to carry out the work, it will remove its 'compulsory' nature and a violation of this Article would be unlikely.

[19] *Van der Mussele v Belgium A.70 (1983) 6 EHRR 163.*

3. For the purpose of this Article the term "forced or compulsory labour" shall not include:

    (a) any work required to be done in the ordinary course of detention imposed according to the provisions of Article 5 of this Convention or during conditional release from such detention;

    (b) any service of a military character or, in case of conscientious objectors in countries where they are recognised, service exacted instead of compulsory military service;

    (c) any service exacted in case of an emergency or calamity threatening the life or well-being of the community;

    (d) any work or service which forms part of normal civic obligations.

ARTICLE 4 (3)(a) -
For the meaning of 'detention' please refer to Article 5.

ARTICLE 4 (3)(b) -
The term 'military service' includes both compulsory military service and that of a voluntary nature. [20]

Recognition of conscientious objection is a choice that is left to the individual states.

ARTICLE 4 (3)(c) -
This section permits the state to take control of emergency situations and, if the need arises, to impose compulsory work upon its citizens.

[20] *Applications 3435-3438/67 W,X,Y and Z v UK 11 YB 562 (1968).*

ARTICLE 4 (3)(d) -

'Normal civic obligations'
The Court of Human Rights and the Commission have not specifically defined this term. However, it appears to involve obligations that come within the boundaries of ordinary citizenship, for example filling in tax documents.

ARTICLE 5

Right to liberty and security

1. Everyone has the right to liberty and security of person. No one shall be deprived of his liberty save in the following cases and in accordance with a procedure prescribed by law:

ARTICLE 5 - RIGHT TO LIBERTY AND SECURITY

ARTICLE 5 (1)

'Liberty and security'
The principal purpose of Article 5 is to protect the citizen from arbitrary arrest and detention by the state. Of course, the right to liberty cannot be absolute and Article 5(1)(a-f) permit the state to arrest and detain an individual in certain specified circumstances.

Article 5 applies to deprivation of physical liberty. It does not apply to lesser restrictions on the liberty of the individual. For example, where the state requires persons to register where one lives, traffic regulations, curfews during civil unrest.

The word 'security' has not been independently defined. Therefore, there is no significant difference in the meaning of the two words.

The six situations listed are the only exceptions permitted; states cannot add to the list.

'In accordance with a procedure prescribed by law'
This means that the arrest and detention must conform to procedure that is contained within domestic law which is accessible and precise. In terms of the procedure, the individual states are afforded a 'margin of appreciation' or discretion as to what particular measures will be implemented.

However, certain over-riding principles must be recognised. Therefore, the domestic procedure must guard against arbitrary and disproportionate action by the state authorities.

(a) the lawful detention of a person after conviction by a competent court;

ARTICLE - 5 (1)(a)

'Detention of a person after conviction by a competent court'
Obviously, this exception allows the courts to impose terms of imprisonment upon offenders who have been found guilty of a criminal offence. Further, the state can detain an individual even if he has lodged an appeal against his conviction. Similarly, a detention will not be retroactively unlawful if his conviction or sentence is overturned on appeal.

'Competent court' means a judicial body independent of the Executive and with the jurisdiction to hear the case.

(b) the lawful arrest or detention of a person for non-compliance with the lawful order of a court or in order to secure the fulfilment of any obligation prescribed by law;

ARTICLE - 5(1)(b)

For the meaning of 'lawful arrest and detention'

See above at Article 5 (1)

'The lawful order of a court'
Examples would include the non-payment of a fine, refusing to undergo a medical examination or an injunction that has been ordered by the court.

'Any obligation prescribed by law'
The Court of Human Rights has stated that this exception applies;

'where the law permits detention of a person to compel him to fulfil a specific and concrete obligation, which he has until then failed to satisfy.' [21]

---

[21] *Engel v Netherlands Series A no.22 1976 1 EHRR 647.*

(c) the lawful arrest or detention of a person effected for the purpose of bringing him before the competent legal authority on reasonable suspicion of having committed an offence or when it is reasonably considered necessary to prevent his committing an offence or fleeing after having done so;

ARTICLE - 5 (1)(c)

For the meaning of 'lawful arrest and detention'

See Article 5.1 above

'Competent legal authority'
In England, Wales and Northern Ireland the 'competent legal authority' that deals with the first hearings at which the accused person will appear is the magistrates' court. In Scotland, it is the District court and the Sheriff court.

'Reasonable suspicion'
In exercising the power to effect an arrest and detention the police or other state authority must only act on 'reasonable suspicion'. The Court of Human Rights has defined reasonable suspicion as arising from 'facts or information which would satisfy an objective observer that the person concerned may have committed the offence.' [22]

'Offence'
Offence means a criminal offence.

---

[22] *Fox, Campbell and Hartley v UK A.182 (1990) 13 EHRR 157.*

(d) the detention of a minor by lawful order for the purpose of educational supervision or his lawful detention for the purpose of bringing him before the competent legal authority;

ARTICLE - 5(1)(d)

'Minor'
The age of majority in the UK is eighteen years.

'Educational supervision'
The authorities are permitted to detain a person under the age of eighteen in order to supervise his education. The detention must be subject to 'a procedure prescribed by law'. As stated above, in addition to national law procedures the authorities are required to accord with the over-riding principles of the Convention, particularly necessity and proportionality.

'Educational purpose' has been interpreted narrowly. The institution where the minor is detained must have educational facilities and trained staff.

(e) the lawful detention of persons for the prevention of the spreading of infectious diseases, of persons of unsound mind, alcoholics or drug addicts or vagrants;

ARTICLE 5 - (1)(e)

This seemingly wide reaching section is again subject to procedures which are 'prescribed by law'. In essence, the detention must be lawful (see Article 5(1)) and this pre-requisite is strengthened by Article 5(4) that enables individuals to have the lawfulness of the detention determined by a court. Most cases under this Article have involved the detention of persons in psychiatric hospitals.

'Unsound mind'

Firstly, the person must be "reliably shown" to be of unsound mind. This means that objective medical expertise must be considered. Secondly, the nature or degree of the mental disorder must be such as to justify the deprivation of liberty. Thirdly, continued confinement is only valid as long as the disorder persists. [23]

[23] *Winterwerp v Netherlands A.33 (1979) 2 EHRR 387. Commn.Report 15th December 1977 paras. 73-78.*

(f) the lawful arrest or detention of a person to prevent his effecting an unauthorised entry into the country or of a person against whom action is being taken with a view to deportation or extradition.

ARTICLE - 5(1)(f)

Article 5(1)(f) allows an individual state the right to deprive a person of his liberty if he is attempting to enter the country without authority. Further, the person can be detained whilst proceedings are taken that will determine the issues of deportation or extradition. The Convention itself does not legislate on the migration of persons between states. Immigration control remains the responsibility of the individual states.

For the meaning of 'lawful arrest and detention' see Article 5(1)

2. Everyone who is arrested shall be informed promptly, in a language which he understands, of the reasons for his arrest and of any charge against him.

ARTICLES - 5 (2) TO 5 (4)

Articles 5(2) to 5(5) set out procedural safeguards which must be adhered to by the state authorities.

ARTICLE - 5 (2)

'Informed promptly'

The arrested person should be informed of the legal and factual grounds for his arrest, whether at one time or in stages, within a sufficient period following his arrest.

If there is a delay of a few hours between the time of the arrest and the giving of the information concerning the charge, the situation is unlikely to violate Article 5(2). [24]

A delay of ten days has been held to violate Article 5(2).

'In a language he understands'

The detainee must be told 'in simple, non-technical language that he can understand, the essential legal and factual grounds for his arrest so as to be able, if he sees fit, to apply to a court to challenge its lawfulness.' [25]

If a foreign person is arrested, the officer or agent must provide an interpreter as soon as possible.

---

[24] *Murray Judgment 28.10.94 Series A no. 300-A*

[25] *Fox, Campbell and Hartley v UK (1990) 13 EHRR 157.*

3. Everyone arrested or detained in accordance with the provisions of paragraph 1(c) of this Article shall be brought promptly before a judge or other officer authorised by law to exercise judicial power and shall be entitled to trial within a reasonable time or to release pending trial. Release may be conditioned by guarantees to appear for trial.

ARTICLE - 5(3)

This section safeguards the detainee's right to appear before a judge promptly. It is the first opportunity for a detainee to challenge the lawfulness of his arrest and detention before an independent judge or officer.

'Promptly'

The period that is set in most European countries is between twenty-four and forty-eight hours. The time limits are a matter for national legislation and the Court of Human Rights and the Commission have not set specific time limits.

In England and Wales, the defendant must be brought before the magistrates' court as soon as is practicable and in any event not later than the first sitting after he is charged with the offence.

'Judge or other officer authorised by law to exercise judicial power'

' Under Article 5(3), there is both a procedural and a substantive requirement. The procedural requirement places the "officer" under the obligation of hearing himself the individual brought before him; the substantive requirement imposes on him the obligations of reviewing the circumstances militating for or against his detention, of deciding, by reference to legal criteria, whether there are reasons to justify detention and of ordering release if there are no such reasons.' [26]

The court with jurisdiction to hear first appearances of an accused person in England, Wales and Northern Ireland is the magistrates' court whilst in Scotland it is the District and Sheriff court. If bail is refused, the accused may appeal to a judge in the Crown Court or the High Court. In Scotland, the accused may appeal the decision at the court that made the original decision and at the High Court of Justiciary.

'Entitled to trial within a reasonable time'

This right ensures that an accused person is not kept in custody for an indefinite period of time. The requirements of 'reasonable time' vary and practices differ between countries. The Court of Human Rights and the Commission have not set specific time limits. The following factors have been considered in ascertaining whether the length of detention has been reasonable:

- *the actual length of the detention;*

- *the length of detention on remand in relation to the nature of the offence;*

- *the penalty prescribed and to be expected in the case of conviction;*

- *material, moral or other matters effecting the detained person;*

- *the conduct of the accused;*

- *the manner in which the investigation was conducted;*

- *the conduct of the judicial authorities concerned.*

---

[26] *Schiesser Judgment 4.12.79 Series A no.34 p.13-14.*

'Release pending trial'

Essentially, this section deals with the issue of bail. This means the release of the accused before his trial. At this point of the process reasonable suspicion that the accused committed the offence is no longer sufficient to justify detention. There must exist relevant and sufficient public interest reasons to justify detention since an accused person is presumed innocent until proven guilty.[27] There are four acceptable justifications for detention before trial;

i. *a risk that the accused person will not appear for trial;*

ii. *a risk that the accused person will interfere with the course of justice;*

iii. *to prevent the accused person from committing further offences;*

iv. *to preserve public order.*

'Release may be conditioned by guarantees to appear for trial'

This means that the court may impose certain conditions upon the accused before granting bail. Examples include:

— *surrender of an individual's passport;*

— *a condition to reside at a particular address or at a bail hostel;*

— *provision of a sum of money as surety or security.*

[27] *Letellier v France A.207 (1991) 14 EHRR 83*

---

4. Everyone who is deprived of his liberty by arrest or detention shall be entitled to take proceedings by which the lawfulness of his detention shall be decided speedily by a court and his release ordered if the detention is not lawful.

ARTICLE - 5 (4)

This section gives the detainee the right to challenge the lawfulness of his arrest and detention.

Further, two obligations are placed upon the state. Firstly, to ensure that the accused is entitled to actually take proceedings in order to challenge the lawfulness of his arrest and detention in a court. Secondly, to ensure release of the detainee if the finding of the court is that the arrest and detention are unlawful.

In English law, this procedural guarantee is known as the right to habeas corpus.

At such a hearing the burden of proving the lawfulness of the detention lies upon the state.

'Entitled to take proceedings'

The accused must be afforded the full benefit of the principle of 'equality of arms', receive a fair hearing and his argument heard in full. If necessary, he should be afforded legal representation.

Furthermore, the accused must be able to request a review of the legality of the detention at reasonable intervals.

'Court'

The court must be independent of the Executive. It must be able to exercise a full range of powers that include decision making on detention on the grounds of law and fact and the power to order the release of the individual where the state fails to support its case for detention.

'Speedily'

No specific time limit has been set. However, the period must not be 'unreasonably long'. Each case will be judged on its specific facts. Factors that will be considered include the diligence of the national authorities and delays caused by the accused.

'Lawful' in Article 5(4)

Certain strict legal procedures must be in place;

Generally Article 5(4) requires that the detained person or his representative be permitted to participate in an oral hearing.

The detained person must be entitled to legal assistance.

The principle of 'equality of arms' applies. Therefore the detainee should be entitled to have access to the official file when challenging the legality of his detention.

The detainee must be told the reasons for his detention in order that he can have the right time and facilities to properly challenge the legality of the state's actions.

The over-riding principles of Convention law require that the detention must not be arbitrary and must be proportionate to the legitimate aim.

5. Everyone who has been the victim of arrest or detention in contravention of the provisions of this Article shall have an enforceable right to compensation.

ARTICLE – 5 (5)

This section safeguards an individual's right to make a claim for compensation in the civil courts against the state authority if his arrest and/or detention was unlawful.

ARTICLE 6

Right to a fair trial

1. In the determination of his civil rights and obligations or of any criminal charge against him, everyone is entitled to a fair and public hearing within a reasonable time by an independent and impartial tribunal established by law. Judgment shall be pronounced publicly but the press and public may be excluded from all or part of the trial in the interest of morals, public order or national security in a democratic society, where the interests of juveniles or the protection of the private life of the parties so require, or to the extent strictly necessary in the opinion of the court in special circumstances where publicity would prejudice the interests of justice.

ARTICLE 6 - RIGHT TO A FAIR TRIAL

'Civil rights and obligations'
The word 'civil' indicates that this section protects rights and obligations in private law.

'Criminal charge'
Defined as 'the official notification given to an individual by the competent authority of an allegation that he has committed a criminal offence.'[28]

The Court of Human Rights expanded the definition to include;

'other measures which carry the implication of such an allegation and which likewise substantially affect the situation of the suspect.'

This expansion on the concept includes actions such as the issue of a warrant or search of a person's premises.

'Fair hearing'
The requirement of 'fairness' is fundamental. In relation to judicial hearings fairness is often described by reference to the 'equality of arms' principle. This means that both sides should be given an equal opportunity to present their case.

An individual must be given personal and reasonable notice of an administrative decision that interferes with his civil rights and obligations, so that he has adequate time to challenge it in court. Accordingly, he must be granted a right of effective access to a court.

The minimum guarantees set out at Article 6 (3) (a) to (e) are not exhaustive.

---

[28] *Eckle v Federal Republic of Germany 15th July 1982 Series A no.51 p.33 para. 73*

Examples of unfairness may include;

– *lack of equality between the parties;*

– *an unfair, imbalanced or inaccurate summing up by the judge;*

– *an unfair press campaign against the accused;*

– *where the defendant is deprived of necessary information which would enable him to challenge a witness's credibility;*

– *where the accused is denied the right to remain silent and not incriminate himself;*

– *where the accused is tried in his absence without his consent;*

– *where the tribunal is biased and lacking in the requisite impartiality;*

– *where no reasoned judgment is given to the accused though this requirement does not apply to jury trial.*

'Public hearing'
Public hearings ensure against proceedings held in secrecy and facilitate access to information.

The parties in the hearing may be heard privately if they consent.

A public hearing at appeal proceedings is not required in all circumstances providing that the trial of the issue was held in public.

As stated in Article 6(1) there are exceptional situations where the public and press may be excluded.

'Reasonable time'
No specific time limits have been set. Each case will be judged on its particular circumstances. Certain factors will be considered including;

- *the complexity of the case;*

- *the conduct of the applicant;*

- *the conduct of the competent, administrative and judicial authorities.*

'Independent and impartial tribunal'
Independent of the Executive, the tribunal must be competent to take legally binding decisions. Further, the tribunal must be free of any prejudice or bias.

2. Everyone charged with a criminal offence shall be presumed innocent until proved guilty according to law.

ARTICLE 6 (2)

The Court of Human Rights has stated in relation to the presumption of innocence;
'When carrying out their duties, the members of a court should not start with the preconceived idea that the accused has committed the offence charged; the burden of proof is on the prosecution, and any doubt should benefit the accused. It also follows that it is for the prosecution to inform the accused of the case that will be made against him, so that he may prepare and present his defence accordingly, and to adduce evidence sufficient to convict him.'

3. Everyone charged with a criminal offence has the following minimum rights:

   (a) to be informed promptly, in a language which he understands and in detail, of the nature and cause of the accusation against him;

ARTICLE 6 (3)

For the meaning of 'promptly' and 'language' see commentary at Article 5(2)
This section places a duty on the state to inform the accused person at an early stage the nature of the offence that he is facing. At this point, the state authorities do not have to give evidence to the accused but they must state material facts that support the charge.

   (b) to have adequate time and facilities for the preparation of his defence;

In harmony with the 'equality of arms' principle, this provision expressly requires that the defence are afforded equality in terms of preparation.

Examples include;

— *time to consider results of the state's investigations which are disclosed to the defendant;*

— *time to consult with his legal representative;*

— *facilities which enable the defendant to consult with his legal representative in private.*

(c) to defend himself in person or through legal assistance of his own choosing or, if he has not sufficient means to pay for legal assistance, to be given it free when the interests of justice so require;

In line with the principle of 'equality of arms' the defendant is afforded certain options in relation to representation.

He is entitled to defend himself. However, the court may limit this right if the case is complex.

Alternatively, he may seek legal representation of his own choosing.

Legal Aid
The second part of Article 6.3 refers to legal aid which is financial assistance to cover the costs of legal representation.

Legal aid is granted subject to the financial means of the defendant and must be in the interests of justice. The following criteria is considered;

– *the capacity of the defendant to represent himself;*

– *the complexity of the case;*

– *the severity of the potential sentence.* [29]

[29] *Granger v UK (1990) 12 EHRR 469, Quaranta v Switzerland (1991) Series A no. 205.*

(d) to examine or have examined witnesses against him and to obtain the attendance and examination of witnesses on his behalf under the same conditions as witnesses against him;

In line with the "equality of arms" principle, this section allows the defendant to cross examine witnesses against him and to call witnesses in support of his case at trial.

(e) to have the free assistance of an interpreter if he cannot understand or speak the language used in court.

> *This provision is self explanatory but it is important to add that the defendant may use the interpreter in order to understand " all those documents or statements in the proceedings…in order to have the benefit of a fair trial." [30]*
>
> ---
>
> [30] *Luedicke, Belkacem and Koc v Federal Republic of Germany 28th November 1978 Series A no. 29.*

ARTICLE 7

No punishment without law

1. No one shall be held guilty of any criminal offence on account of any act or omission which did not constitute a criminal offence under national or international law at the time when it was committed. Nor shall a heavier penalty be imposed than the one that was applicable at the time the criminal offence was committed.

> **ARTICLE 7 – NO PUNISHMENT WITHOUT LAW**
>
> *Article 7 (1) lays down two prohibitions. The first prohibits the retroactive application of a criminal offence. This means that the state cannot impose any punishment on conduct that was not classified as criminal when the act or omission occurred.*
>
> *The principle falls directly in line with the concept of fairness. It is essential that the law is accessible and precise in order that the citizen can know what conduct is classified as criminal. This requires that "the offence should be clearly described by law." [31]*
>
> *The second element of Article 7 (1) prohibits the state from retroactively increasing a penalty upon an accused person.*
>
> ---
>
> [31] *Handyside v UK (1974) 17 YB 228*

2. This Article shall not prejudice the trial and punishment of any person for any act or omission which, at the time when it was committed, was criminal according to the general principles of law recognised by civilised nations.

> *Article 7(2) provides an exception meaning that Article 7(1) would not affect laws that were passed at the end of the Second World War to punish war crimes, treason and collaboration with the enemy.*

ARTICLE 8

Right to respect for private and family life

1. Everyone has the right to respect for his private and family life, his home and his correspondence.

ARTICLE 8 - RIGHT TO RESPECT FOR PRIVATE AND FAMILY LIFE

'right to respect'

The Court of Human Rights has established that the state has a dual responsibility in terms of the right to respect family life:

'Although the object of Article 8 is essentially that of protecting the individual against arbitrary interference by the public authorities, it does not merely compel the state to abstain from such interference: in addition to this primarily negative undertaking, there must be positive obligations inherent in an effective respect for private and family life.' [32]

'private life'

'The right to respect for "private life" is the right to privacy, the right to live as far as one wishes, protected from publicity… It comprises also, to a certain degree, the right to establish and develop relationships with other human beings especially in the emotional field, for the development and fulfilment of one's own personality.' [33]

However, the Court has limited the scope of the right;

'The claim to respect for private life is automatically reduced to the extent that the individual himself brings his private life into contact with public life or into close connection with other protected interests.' [34]

---

[32] *Airey v Ireland (1979) Series A no.32 p.17 para.32*

[33] *Van Oosterwijk v Belgium(Comm. Rep. 1979)*

[34] *Bruggemann and Schaeuten v Federal Republic of Germany Commn.Report 12ᵗʰ July 1977.*

'Family life'
'Family' has been given a wide interpretation by the Court of Human Rights. In addition to the formal relationships such as husband and wife and parent and child, relationships where there is a sufficient personal tie will be included.

Examples of such relationships include;

– *siblings;*

– *uncle and nephew;*

– *grandparent and grandchild;*

– *couples in a current relationship;*

– *child and foster parents.*

'Respect for the home'
The citizen has the right to occupy his home and not to be expelled from it.[35]

'Respect for correspondence'
'Correspondence' applies to written and telephone communications.

The right to have a person's 'correspondence' respected is concerned principally with protecting the position of detainees.

A prisoner must be able to correspond with his legal representative or a judicial body for only then can he protect his rights.

Some restrictions have been permitted in relation to matters of security.

[35] *Cyprus v Turkey (1976) 4 EHRR 282*

2. There shall be no interference by a public authority with the exercise of this right except such as is in accordance with the law and is necessary in a democratic society in the interests of national security, public safety or the economic well-being of the country, for the prevention of disorder or crime, for the protection of health or morals, or for the protection of the rights and freedoms of others.

ARTICLE 8(2)
The state may rely on specific grounds in order to 'interfere' with the Article 8.1 guarantee. The purpose of the exceptions is to enable the state to balance the rights of the individual with the broader interests of society as a whole in instances where they conflict.

A state can only interfere with the fundamental right within the confines of the specific exceptions listed in the second paragraph. [36]

The exceptions will be subject to strict interpretation;

'Strict interpretation means that no other criteria than those mentioned in the exception clause itself may be at the basis of any restrictions, and these criteria, in turn, must be understood in such a way that the language is not extended beyond its ordinary meaning.' [37]

In addition, the conditions of 'lawfulness' and 'necessary in a democratic society' must receive strict application.

'In accordance with law'

This prerequisite is the starting point in an analysis of state action under one of the exceptions. If the Court find that the action was not lawful, it will find a violation and proceed no further. On the other hand, if the action was found to be 'in accordance with law', the Court will go on to examine whether the action was 'necessary in a democratic society.'

'Law' means all forms of domestic law.

The Court of Human Rights and the Commission have stated;

'Firstly, the law must be adequately accessible: the citizen must be able to have an indication that is in the circumstances of the legal rules in a given case. Secondly, a norm cannot be regarded as a "law" unless it is formulated with sufficient precision to enable the citizen to regulate his conduct.' [38]

Therefore, the citizen must be able to access the particular law which must be available in precise form.

The Court has added;

'the law must indicate the scope of any such discretion conferred on the competent authorities and the manner of its exercise with sufficient clarity, having regard to the legitimate aim of the measures in question, to give the individual adequate protection against arbitrary interference.' [39]

---

[36] *Vagrancy cases (1991), Golder v UK (1975)*

[37] *Sunday Times Judgment Commn. Report 18th May 1977 paras.194-195*

[38] *Sunday Times Judgment Series A no.30 p.31 para.49*

[39] *Malone Judgment 2nd August 1984 Series A no.82 p.33 para 6.*

> **'Necessary in a democratic society'**
> *Essentially, the state is afforded considerable discretion as to what is necessary. This is often referred to as a state's margin of appreciation.*
>
> *The Court of Human Rights has stated;*
>
> *'By reason of their direct and continuous contact with the vital forces of their countries, state authorities are in principle in a better position than the international judge to give an opinion on the exact content of these requirements…as well as on the "necessity" of a "restriction" or "penalty" intended to meet them.'* [40]
>
> *However, the Court of Human Rights has also stated that the margin of appreciation afforded to states is subject to supervision.*
>
> *A two-stage process is adopted when examining whether an action was 'necessary'. Firstly, whether the aim of the state action had a legitimate purpose. Secondly, whether the means used was "proportionate to the legitimate aim pursued."* [41]
>
> ---
>
> [40] *Handyside v UK (1976) 1 EHRR 737*
>
> [41] *Golder and Silver, Dudgeon v UK (1981), Norris v Ireland (1988).*

ARTICLE 9

Freedom of thought, conscience and religion

1. Everyone has the right to freedom of thought, conscience and religion; this right includes freedom to change his religion or belief and freedom, either alone or in community with others and in public or private, to manifest his religion or belief, in worship, teaching, practice and observance.

2. Freedom to manifest one's religion or beliefs shall be subject only to such limitations as are prescribed by law and are necessary in a democratic society in the interests of public safety, for the protection of public order, health or morals, or for the protection of the rights and freedoms of others.

> **ARTICLE 9 – FREEDOM OF THOUGHT, CONSCIENCE AND RELIGION**
> *The guarantee set out in Article 9.1 protects the right of the citizen to hold opinions without any indoctrination or restraint being imposed by the state.*
>
> *Article 9(1) establishes safeguards ensuring respect and protection for all varieties of belief and worship.*
>
> *'Community with others' means that a church or organisation may claim that their rights have been infringed.*

The right of the state to interfere is limited and it would have to justify its actions under the criteria in Article 9(2).

For the meaning of 'prescribed by law' and 'necessary in a democratic society'

Please see comments under Article 8(2)

ARTICLE 10

Freedom of expression

1. Everyone has the right to freedom of expression. This right shall include freedom to hold opinions and to receive and impart information and ideas without interference by public authority and regardless of frontiers. This Article shall not prevent States from requiring the licensing of broadcasting, television or cinema enterprises.

2. The exercise of these freedoms, since it carries with it duties and responsibilities, may be subject to such formalities, conditions, restrictions or penalties as are prescribed by law and are necessary in a democratic society, in the interests of national security, territorial integrity or public safety, for the prevention of disorder or crime, for the protection of health or morals, for the protection of the reputation or rights of others, for preventing the disclosure of information received in confidence, or for maintaining the authority and impartiality of the judiciary.

ARTICLE 10 – FREEDOM OF EXPRESSION
Article 10 extends the effect of Article 9 for it guarantees the expression and receipt of opinions and ideas.

'Everyone'
'Everyone' applies to organisations and companies as well as individuals.

'Freedom of expression'
'Freedom of expression constitutes one of the most essential foundations of such a society, one of the basic conditions for its progress and for the development of every man… It is applicable not only to "information" or "ideas" that are favourably received or regarded as inoffensive or as a matter of indifference, but also to those that offend, shock or disturb the state or any sector of the population. Such are the demands of that pluralism, tolerance and broadmindedness without which there is no "democratic society".' [34]

[34] *Handyside v UK A.24 (1976) 1 EHRR 737.*

'Receive information'
The State is not permitted to prevent or restrict a person from receiving information that others may wish or may be willing to give. However, the State itself will not be under an obligation to supply information.

'Interference'
The Court of Human Rights has stated that if a person agrees or contracts to limit their freedom of expression it is unlikely that a violation would occur.

For the meaning of 'prescribed by law' and 'necessary in a democratic society'

Please see the commentary at Article 8(2)

'National security'
Permitted restrictions by the state under this heading have included:

— *An interlocutory injunction restraining newspapers from publishing information that was contained in a book written by a former member of the security services.*

— *Government restrictions placed upon broadcasters preventing items of news relating to organisations connected with and supporting terrorism.*

'Rights of others'
Clearly a balance must be achieved which serves to protect the rights of others. The restrictions may aim at protecting rights of reputation and religion.

An example that illustrates such a protection arose in the Otto E.F.A. Remer v Germany case (1995)[35] that centred on a conviction which had been imposed on an eighty year old man for incitement to racial hatred. The party concerned published material denying the existence of gas chambers in Nazi concentration camps. It was held that the action taken by the authorities was necessary in a democratic society for the protection of the reputation or rights of others.

'Maintaining the authority and impartiality of the judiciary'
This exception reflects the principle of 'fairness' in legal proceedings. The courts may prohibit the publication of information about the proceedings in order to prevent the effect of prejudicial material.

---

[35] *Appln. 25096/94. Otto EFA Remer v Germany 82-A DR 117(1995).*

ARTICLE 11

Freedom of assembly and association

1. Everyone has the right to freedom of peaceful assembly and to freedom of association with others, including the right to form and to join trade unions for the protection of his interests.

2. No restrictions shall be placed on the exercise of these rights other than such as are prescribed by law and are necessary in a democratic society in the interests of national security or public safety, for the prevention of disorder or crime, for the protection of health or morals or for the protection of the rights and freedoms of others. This Article shall not prevent the imposition of lawful restrictions on the exercise of these rights by members of the armed forces, of the police or of the administration of the State.

ARTICLE 11 - FREEDOM OF ASSEMBLY AND ASSOCIATION

'Peaceful assembly'

The wording of Article 11(1) allows the authorities to apply the condition that the assembly be peaceful. If it is reasonably believed that the assembly will not be peaceful then the state authority will be entitled to prevent it.

The Court of Human Rights has stated;

'The right of peaceful assembly …is a fundamental right in a democratic society and…one of the foundations of such a society…As such this covers both private and public meetings and meetings in thoroughfares. Where the latter is concerned, their subjection to an authorisation procedure does not normally encroach upon the essence of the right. Such procedures in keeping with the requirements of Article 11.1, if only that the authorities may be in a position to ensure the peaceful nature of a meeting, and accordingly does not as such constitute interference with the exercise of the right.' [36]

---

[36] *Appln. No.8191/78*

Violent counter demonstrations
'The right to freedom of peaceful assembly is secured to everyone who has the intention of organising a peaceful demonstration.... The possibility of violent counter-demonstrations, or the possibility of extremists with violent intentions, not members of the organising association, joining the demonstration cannot as such take away that right. Even if there is a real risk of a public procession resulting in disorder by developments outside the control of those organising it, such procession does not for this reason alone fall outside the scope of Article 11.1 of the Convention, but any restriction placed on such an assembly must be in conformity with the terms of paragraph 2 of that provision.' [37]

'Freedom of association'
An association is regarded as more formal and more organised than an assembly. The court has stated 'that the term "association" presupposes a voluntary grouping for a common goal.' [38]

'The right to join trade unions'
This right also implies the right not to associate with or not to be affiliated with a trade union.

For the meaning of 'prescribed by law' and 'necessary in a democratic society'

Please see the commentary at Article 8(2)

[37] *Appln. No.8440/78*

[38] *Webster v UK Comm.Rep.1979*

ARTICLE 12

Right to marry

Men and women of marriageable age have the right to marry and to found a family, according to the national laws governing the exercise of this right.

ARTICLE 12 - RIGHT TO MARRY

'Marriageable age'
The minimum age for marriage is a matter for national law. In the United Kingdom marriageable age is currently sixteen.

'According to the national laws'

The Commission has stated that measures that regulate the fundamental right "must not injure the substance of the right." [39]

'Such laws may thus lay down formal rules concerning matters such as notice, publicity and the formalities whereby marriage is solemnised…They may also lay down rules of substance based on generally recognised considerations of public interest . Examples are rules concerning capacity, consent, prohibited degrees of consanguinity or the prevention of bigamy. However .national law may not otherwise deprive a person or category of persons of full legal capacity of the right to marry. Nor may it substantially interfere with their exercise of the right.' [40]

'Right to marry'

The right to marry under Article 12 does not include the right to divorce in order to re-marry.

'To found a family'

Essentially this protects citizens from arbitrary programmes of compulsory sterilisation or other population control measures being imposed by the state.

The right does not guarantee the right to have children born out of wedlock. Article 12 foresees the right to marry and to found a family as one single right.

---

[39] *Hamer v UK Comm.Report 13.12.79 para 62*

[40] *Hamer v UK Comm.Report 13.12.79 para 62*

ARTICLE 14

Prohibition of discrimination

The enjoyment of the rights and freedoms set forth in this Convention shall be secured without discrimination on any ground such as sex, race, colour, language, religion, political or other opinion, national or social origin, association with a national minority, property, birth or other status.

ARTICLE 14 - PROHIBITION OF DISCRIMINATION

Article 14 does not set down a general prohibition on discrimination. It aims at ensuring that the rights contained within the Convention are secured without discrimination.

Therefore, it does not operate independently and is regarded as having an accessory nature. It operates in conjunction with the other Articles of the Convention. However, if it is found that a state has complied with the other Article, it may still be found that Article 14 has been violated.

Article 14 gives examples of established areas of discrimination but the list is not limited. This section applies to discrimination 'on any ground' i.e. where there is a difference of treatment between persons who are similarly situated.

'Discrimination'
'The notion of discrimination within the meaning of Article 14 includes in general cases where a person or group is treated, without proper justification, less favourably than another, even though the more favourable treatment is not called for by the Convention.' [41]

Therefore, a state will be able to defend the differential treatment if it has an objective and reasonable justification.

---

[41] *Abdulaziz, Cabales and Balkandali v UK (1985) 7 EHRR 471.*

ARTICLE 16

Restrictions on political activity of aliens

Nothing in Articles 10, 11 and 14 shall be regarded as preventing the High Contracting Parties from imposing restrictions on the political activity of aliens.

ARTICLE 16 - RESTRICTIONS ON POLITICAL ACTIVITY OF ALIENS.
This provision allows states to impose restrictions on aliens which is in addition to the limitations and restrictions incorporated in Articles 10 (Expression), 11 (Assembly) and 14 (Discrimination). However, the Article focuses specifically on 'political activity.'

ARTICLE 17

Prohibition of abuse of rights

Nothing in this Convention may be interpreted as implying for any State, group or person any right to engage in any activity or perform any act aimed at the destruction of any of the rights and freedoms set forth herein or at their limitation to a greater extent than is provided for in the Convention.

ARTICLE 17 - PROHIBITION OF ABUSE OF RIGHTS
Article 17 prevents a state, group or person from interpreting the Convention in such a way as to ultimately destroy or limit the Convention rights.

ARTICLE 18

Limitation on use of restrictions on rights

The restrictions permitted under this Convention to the said rights and freedoms shall not be applied for any purpose other than those for which they have been prescribed.

ARTICLE 18 - LIMITATIONS ON USE OF RESTRICTIONS ON RIGHTS
Article 18 prohibits misuse of the permitted exceptions contained within the Convention.

PART II

THE FIRST PROTOCOL

ARTICLE 1

Protection of property

Every natural or legal person is entitled to the peaceful enjoyment of his possessions. No one shall be deprived of his possessions except in the public interest and subject to the conditions provided for by law and by the general principles of international law.

The preceding provisions shall not, however, in any way impair the right of a State to enforce such laws as it deems necessary to control the use of property in accordance with the general interest or to secure the payment of taxes or other contributions or penalties.

PART II

THE FIRST PROTOCOL

'Every natural and legal person'
This Article expressly protects individuals and legal persons, such as organisations and companies.

'Possessions'

The concept of 'possessions' has been given a wide interpretation and application. It covers the normal terms used in private property law. However, it does not include the right to acquire property. Possession does extend to non-physical property as is illustrated in the following list of examples;

– *movable and immovable property*

– *tangible and intangible property*

– *shares*

– *patents*

– *an entitlement to use property*

– *a benefit resulting from a restrictive covenant*

– *an entitlement to an annual rent*

– *an economic interest connected to the running of a business*

– *the right to exercise a profession*

– *a legal claim (provided it is concrete and adequately specified).*

The claimant must be able to establish the nature of his property right and his entitlement to enjoy it under national law.

'Deprivation of possessions' and 'control the use of property' and 'public interest'

In terms of all the circumstances whereby the state can interfere with property, the authorities enjoy the benefit of a wide margin of appreciation. Essentially, this means that the national legislatures are afforded distinct width of freedom in terms of the determination and implementation of social and economic policies.

The decisions of the national legislatures will not be interfered with unless it is perceived that a decision taken by such a body is manifestly without reasonable foundation.

Importantly, a fair balance must be sought and attained between the general interest of the community and the rights of the individual.

The meaning of 'subject to the conditions provided for by law and by the general principles of international law'

Essentially the state authorities must comply with domestic legal procedures. Such procedures must be adequately accessible and precise.

The principles contained in Article 6 must be complied with in addition to the other Convention legal principles such as proportionality and necessity.

ARTICLE 2

Right to education

No person shall be denied the right to education. In the exercise of any functions which it assumes in relation to education and to teaching, the State shall respect the right of parents to ensure such education and teaching in conformity with their own religious and philosophical convictions.

ARTICLE 2 - RIGHT TO EDUCATION

'The right to education'

' *The negative formulation (of the right to education) indicates…that the Contracting Parties do not recognise such a right to education as would require them to establish at their own expense, or to subsidise, education of any particular type or at any particular level.'*

' *All member states of the Council of Europe…possess a general and official educational system. There (is not) therefore, any question of requiring each State to establish such a system, but merely of guaranteeing to persons subject to the jurisdiction of the Contracting Parties the right, in principle to avail themselves of the means of instruction existing at a given time.'* [42]

The meaning of 'respect the right of parents'

'The second sentence of Article 2 implies on the other hand that the State, in fulfilling the functions assumed by it in regard to education and teaching, must take care that information or knowledge included in the curriculum is conveyed in an objective, critical and pluralistic manner. The State is forbidden to pursue an aim of indoctrination that might be considered as not respecting parents' religious and philosophical convictions. That is the limit that must not be exceeded.' [43]

'Philosophical convictions'

The Court of Human Rights has stated that;

'such convictions as are worthy of respect in a "democratic society"…and are not incompatible with human dignity; in addition, they must not conflict with the fundamental right of the child to education, the whole of Article 2 being dominated by its first line.' [44]

---

[42] *Belgian Linguistic Case (No2)(1968) 1 EHRR 252*

[43] *Kjeldson, Busk, Madsen and Pedersen v Denmark (1976) Series A no.23 p.26 para 53.*

[44] *Campbell and Cosans v UK A48 (1982) 4 EHRR 293.*

ARTICLE 3

Right to free elections

The High Contracting Parties undertake to hold free elections at reasonable intervals by secret ballot, under conditions which will ensure the free expression of the opinion of the people in the choice of the legislature.

ARTICLE 3 - RIGHT TO FREE ELECTIONS
This provision safeguards the system of democracy by placing a positive obligation upon the State to ensure that free elections take place at reasonable intervals.

States are afforded a wide margin of appreciation in terms of what particular electoral system is adopted.

PART III

THE SIXTH PROTOCOL

ARTICLE 1

Abolition of the death penalty

The death penalty shall be abolished. No one shall be condemned to such penalty or executed.

PART III

The Sixth Protocol

Article 1
As a result of its inclusion in the Act, the UK signed the Sixth Protocol on 27 January 1999 and will ratify it in due course. The death penalty was abolished in the UK in 1965, with the exceptions of treason and piracy, which were abolished by section 36 of the Crime and Disorder Act 1998. Despite its abolition, the question of whether the death penalty should be reinstated has arisen on a number of occasions. The effect of the inclusion of the Sixth Protocol is that it will not now be possible to reinstate the death penalty in the UK without renouncing the Convention. A state cannot derogate from or make a reservation to the Sixth Protocol.

ARTICLE 2

Death penalty in time of war

A State may make provision in its law for the death penalty in respect of acts committed in time of war or of imminent threat of war; such penalty shall be applied only in the instances laid down in the law and in accordance with its provisions. The State shall communicate to the Secretary General of the Council of Europe the relevant provisions of that law.

> **Article 2**
> *In times of war or imminent war, a state may make provision for the death penalty.*

SCHEDULE 2

REMEDIAL ORDERS

Orders

1.– (1) A remedial order may-

    (a) contain such incidental, supplemental, consequential or transitional provision as the person making it considers appropriate;

    (b) be made so as to have effect from a date earlier than that on which it is made;

    (c) make provision for the delegation of specific functions;

    (d) make different provision for different cases.

> **SCHEDULE 2**
>
> **REMEDIAL ORDERS**
>
> **Paragraph 1**
> *This paragraph makes further provision in respect of remedial orders under section 10.*
>
> **Subparagraph (1).**
> *The purpose of this subparagraph is to give the Minister making a remedial order the flexibility and discretion to make whatever order is considered necessary in the particular circumstances of each situation of incompatibility. The wide ambit of remedial orders includes supplemental and transitional provisions, delegation of specific functions and retrospective effect. However, remedial orders are subject to the Parliamentary approval procedures in paragraph 2 of Schedule 2.*

(2) The power conferred by sub-paragraph (1)(a) includes-

  (a) power to amend primary legislation (including primary legislation other than that which contains the incompatible provision); and

  (b) power to amend or revoke subordinate legislation (including subordinate legislation other than that which contains the incompatible provision).

Subparagraph (2)
Remedial orders may amend or repeal not only primary and subordinate legislation which is incompatible with Convention rights but also any other primary and subordinate legislation which, although not of itself incompatible, requires amending or revocation as a consequence of the amendments to the incompatible legislation.

(3) A remedial order may be made so as to have the same extent as the legislation which it affects.

Subparagraph (3)
is self explanatory.

(4) No person is to be guilty of an offence solely as a result of the retrospective effect of a remedial order.

Subparagraph (4)
It is a fundamental principle of criminal law, which is specifically protected by Article 7 of the Convention, that persons cannot be found guilty of a criminal offence which did not constitute an offence at the time it was committed. Where a remedial order has retrospective effect under subparagraph (1), a person cannot be guilty of a criminal offence solely as a result of such an order.

Procedure

2. No remedial order may be made unless-

  (a) a draft of the order has been approved by a resolution of each House of Parliament made after the end of the period of 60 days beginning with the day on which the draft was laid; or

(b) it is declared in the order that it appears to the person making it that, because of the urgency of the matter, it is necessary to make the order without a draft being so approved.

Paragraph 2
This paragraph provides that Parliamentary approval must be obtained in respect of remedial orders. Urgent orders can be made without prior Parliamentary approval.

Subparagraphs (a) and (b).
A remedial order cannot be made unless a draft of the order is laid before each House of Parliament and approved by resolution, following a 60 day period for consideration. Where the order is considered urgent, the Minister responsible can make the order without obtaining the prior approval of each House of Parliament. However, in such cases paragraph 4 applies.

Orders laid in draft

3.– (1) No draft may be laid under paragraph 2(a) unless-

(a) the person proposing to make the order has laid before Parliament a document which contains a draft of the proposed order and the required information; and
(b) the period of 60 days, beginning with the day on which the document required by this sub-paragraph was laid, has ended.

Subparagraph (1)
A draft remedial order under paragraph 2 (a) cannot be laid before Parliament unless a document containing the draft order is laid before Parliament, together with an explanation of the incompatibility which the order seeks to remove and particulars of the relevant declaration of incompatibility or finding and a statement of the reasons for proceeding under section 10. Parliament then has a period of 60 days to consider such a document.

(2) If representations have been made during that period, the draft laid under paragraph 2(a) must be accompanied by a statement containing-

(a) a summary of the representations; and
(b) if, as a result of the representations, the proposed order has been changed, details of the changes.

> **Subparagraph (2)**
> *In the event that representations are made during the 60 day period, when the draft order is laid before each House of Parliament under paragraph 2 (a) it must be accompanied by a statement which summarises the representations and details any changes which have been made as a result of the representations.*

Urgent cases

4.– (1) If a remedial order ("the original order") is made without being approved in draft, the person making it must lay it before Parliament, accompanied by the required information, after it is made.

> **Subparagraph (1)**
> *Where an urgent order is made without the prior approval of Parliament in accordance with paragraph 2 (b), the order must be laid before Parliament after it is made, together with an explanation of the incompatibility which the order seeks to remove and particulars of the relevant declaration of incompatibility or other finding and a statement of the reasons for proceeding under section 10.*

(2) If representations have been made during the period of 60 days beginning with the day on which the original order was made, the person making it must (after the end of that period) lay before Parliament a statement containing-

    (a) a summary of the representations; and

    (b) if, as a result of the representations, he considers it appropriate to make changes to the original order, details of the changes.

> **Subparagraph (2)**
> *Parliament then has 60 days to consider the order. If representations are made within the 60 day period, such representations must be summarised in a statement and details of any proposed changes to the order must be contained in the statement.*

(3) If sub-paragraph (2)(b) applies, the person making the statement must-

    (a) make a further remedial order replacing the original order; and

    (b) lay the replacement order before Parliament.

> **Subparagraph (3)**
> *Where proposed changes are made then a further remedial order replacing the original order must be made and placed before Parliament.*

(4) If, at the end of the period of 120 days beginning with the day on which the original order was made, a resolution has not been passed by each House approving the original or replacement order, the order ceases to have effect (but without that affecting anything previously done under either order or the power to make a fresh remedial order).

> **Subparagraph (4)**
> *If each House has not passed a resolution approving the order within 120 days from the date the order was made, the order will cease to have effect. This does not affect anything done while the order was in effect and does not prevent the Minister from making a fresh remedial order.*

Definitions

5. In this Schedule-

    "representations" means representations about a remedial order (or proposed remedial order) made to the person making (or proposing to make) it and includes any relevant Parliamentary report or resolution; and

    "required information" means-

    (a) an explanation of the incompatibility which the order (or proposed order) seeks to remove, including particulars of the relevant declaration, finding or order; and
    (b) a statement of the reasons for proceeding under section 10 and for making an order in those terms.

> **Subparagraph (5)**
> *A remedial order laid before Parliament must be accompanied by a statement which sets out the incompatibility and the reasons why the Minister considers the order appropriate.*

Calculating periods

6. In calculating any period for the purposes of this Schedule, no account is to be taken of any time during which-

(a) Parliament is dissolved or prorogued; or

(b) both Houses are adjourned for more than four days.

Subparagraph (6)
is self explanatory.

SCHEDULE 3

S<small>ECTIONS</small> 14 <small>AND</small> 15.

D<small>EROGATION AND</small> R<small>ESERVATION</small>

P<small>ART</small> I

D<small>EROGATION</small>

The 1988 notification

The United Kingdom Permanent Representative to the Council of Europe presents his compliments to the Secretary General of the Council, and has the honour to convey the following information in order to ensure compliance with the obligations of Her Majesty's Government in the United Kingdom under Article 15(3) of the Convention for the Protection of Human Rights and Fundamental Freedoms signed at Rome on 4 November 1950.

There have been in the United Kingdom in recent years campaigns of organised terrorism connected with the affairs of Northern Ireland which have manifested themselves in activities which have included repeated murder, attempted murder, maiming, intimidation and violent civil disturbance and in bombing and fire raising which have resulted in death, injury and widespread destruction of property. As a result, a public emergency within the meaning of Article 15(1) of the Convention exists in the United Kingdom.

The Government found it necessary in 1974 to introduce and since then, in cases concerning persons reasonably suspected of involvement in terrorism connected with the affairs of Northern Ireland, or of certain offences under the legislation, who have been detained for 48 hours, to exercise powers enabling further detention without charge, for periods of up to five days, on the authority of the Secretary of State. These powers are at present to be found in Section 12 of the Prevention of Terrorism (Temporary Provisions) Act 1984, Article 9 of the Prevention of Terrorism (Supplemental Temporary Provisions) Order 1984 and Article 10 of the Prevention of Terrorism (Supplemental Temporary Provisions) (Northern Ireland) Order 1984.

Section 12 of the Prevention of Terrorism (Temporary Provisions) Act 1984 provides for a person whom a constable has arrested on reasonable grounds of suspecting him to be guilty of an offence under Section 1, 9 or 10 of the Act, or to be or to have been involved in terrorism connected with the affairs of Northern Ireland, to be detained in right of the arrest for up to 48 hours and thereafter, where the Secretary of State extends the detention period, for up to a further five days. Section 12 substantially re-enacted Section 12 of the Prevention of Terrorism (Temporary Provisions) Act 1976 which, in turn, substantially re-enacted Section 7 of the Prevention of Terrorism (Temporary Provisions) Act 1974.

Article 10 of the Prevention of Terrorism (Supplemental Temporary Provisions) (Northern Ireland) Order 1984 (SI 1984/417) and Article 9 of the Prevention of Terrorism (Supplemental Temporary Provisions) Order 1984 (SI 1984/418) were both made under Sections 13 and 14 of and Schedule 3 to the 1984 Act and substantially re-enacted powers of detention in Orders made under the 1974 and 1976 Acts. A person who is being examined under Article 4 of either Order on his arrival in, or on seeking to leave, Northern Ireland or Great Britain for the purpose of determining whether he is or has been involved in terrorism connected with the affairs of Northern Ireland, or whether there are grounds for suspecting that he has committed an offence under Section 9 of the 1984 Act, may be detained under Article 9 or 10, as appropriate, pending the conclusion of his examination. The period of this examination may exceed 12 hours if an examining officer has reasonable grounds for suspecting him to be or to have been involved in acts of terrorism connected with the affairs of Northern Ireland.

Where such a person is detained under the said Article 9 or 10 he may be detained for up to 48 hours on the authority of an examining officer and thereafter, where the Secretary of State extends the detention period, for up to a further five days.

In its judgment of 29 November 1988 in the Case of (Italic)Brogan and Others(Italic), the European Court of Human Rights held that there had been a violation of Article 5(3) in respect of each of the applicants, all of whom had been detained under Section 12 of the 1984 Act. The Court held that even the shortest of the four periods of detention concerned, namely four days and six hours, fell outside the constraints as to time permitted by the first part of Article 5(3). In addition, the Court held that there had been a violation of Article 5(5) in the case of each applicant.

Following this judgment, the Secretary of State for the Home Department informed Parliament on 6 December 1988 that, against the background of the terrorist campaign, and the over-riding need to bring terrorists to justice, the Government did not believe that the maximum period of detention should be reduced. He informed Parliament that the Government were examining the matter with a view to responding to the judgment. On 22 December 1988, the Secretary of State further informed Parliament that it remained the Government's wish, if it could be achieved, to find a judicial process under which extended detention might be reviewed and where appropriate authorised by a judge or other judicial officer. But a further period of reflection and consultation was necessary before the Government could bring forward a firm and final view.

Since the judgment of 29 November 1988 as well as previously, the Government have found it necessary to continue to exercise, in relation to terrorism connected with the affairs of Northern Ireland, the powers described above enabling further detention without charge for periods of up to 5 days, on the authority of the Secretary of State, to the extent strictly required by the exigencies of the situation to enable necessary enquiries and investigations properly to be completed in order to decide whether criminal proceedings should be instituted. To the extent that the exercise of these powers may be inconsistent with the obligations imposed by the Convention the Government has availed itself of the right of derogation conferred by Article 15(1) of the Convention and will continue to do so until further notice.

Dated 23 December 1988.

The 1989 notification

The United Kingdom Permanent Representative to the Council of Europe presents his compliments to the Secretary General of the Council, and has the honour to convey the following information.

In his communication to the Secretary General of 23 December 1988, reference was made to the introduction and exercise of certain powers under section 12 of the Prevention of Terrorism (Temporary Provisions) Act 1984, Article 9 of the Prevention of Terrorism (Supplemental Temporary Provisions) Order 1984 and Article 10 of the Prevention of Terrorism (Supplemental Temporary Provisions) (Northern Ireland) Order 1984.

These provisions have been replaced by section 14 of and paragraph 6 of Schedule 5 to the Prevention of Terrorism (Temporary Provisions) Act 1989, which make comparable provision. They came into force on 22 March 1989. A copy of these provisions is enclosed.

The United Kingdom Permanent Representative avails himself of this opportunity to renew to the Secretary General the assurance of his highest consideration.

23 March 1989.

PART II

RESERVATION

At the time of signing the present (First) Protocol, I declare that, in view of certain provisions of the Education Acts in the United Kingdom, the principle affirmed in the second sentence of Article 2 is accepted by the United Kingdom only so far as it is compatible with the provision of efficient instruction and training, and the avoidance of unreasonable public expenditure.

Dated 20 March 1952. Made by the United Kingdom Permanent Representative to the Council of Europe.

SCHEDULE 4

JUDICIAL PENSIONS

Duty to make orders about pensions

1.– (1) The appropriate Minister must by order make provision with respect to pensions payable to or in respect of any holder of a judicial office who serves as an ECHR judge.

(2) A pensions order must include such provision as the Minister making it considers is necessary to secure that-

    (a) an ECHR judge who was, immediately before his appointment as an ECHR judge, a member of a judicial pension scheme is entitled to remain as a member of that scheme;

(b) the terms on which he remains a member of the scheme are those which would have been applicable had he not been appointed as an ECHR judge; and

(c) entitlement to benefits payable in accordance with the scheme continues to be determined as if, while serving as an ECHR judge, his salary was that which would (but for section 18(4)) have been payable to him in respect of his continuing service as the holder of his judicial office.

Contributions

2. A pensions order may, in particular, make provision-

(a) for any contributions which are payable by a person who remains a member of a scheme as a result of the order, and which would otherwise be payable by deduction from his salary, to be made otherwise than by deduction from his salary as an ECHR judge; and

(b) for such contributions to be collected in such manner as may be determined by the administrators of the scheme.

Amendments of other enactments

3. A pensions order may amend any provision of, or made under, a pensions Act in such manner and to such extent as the Minister making the order considers necessary or expedient to ensure the proper administration of any scheme to which it relates.

Definitions

4. In this Schedule-

"appropriate Minister" means-

(a) in relation to any judicial office whose jurisdiction is exercisable exclusively in relation to Scotland, the Secretary of State; and

(b) otherwise, the Lord Chancellor;

"ECHR judge" means the holder of a judicial office who is serving as a judge of the Court;

"judicial pension scheme" means a scheme established by and in accordance with a pensions Act;

"pensions Act" means-

(a) the County Courts Act (Northern Ireland) 1959;

(b) the Sheriffs' Pensions (Scotland) Act 1961;

(c) the Judicial Pensions Act 1981; or

(d) the Judicial Pensions and Retirement Act 1993; and

"pensions order" means an order made under paragraph 1.

TABLE A

Countries which have signed or ratified the Convention★

Albania	Lithuania
Andorra	Luxembourg
Austria	Malta
Belgium	Moldova
Bulgaria	Netherlands
Cyprus	Norway
Croatia	Poland
Czech Republic	Portugal
Denmark	Romania
Estonia	Russia
Finland	San Marino
France	Slovakia
Germany	Slovenia
Greece	Spain
Hungary	Sweden
Iceland	Switzerland
Ireland	The Former Yugoslav Republic
Italy	of Macedonia
Latvia	Turkey
Lichtenstein	Ukraine
	United Kingdom

★ as of 28 October 1998

The Guide to the Human Rights Act was written by David Leckie, a practising barrister and a member of the Human Rights Group at Hardwicke Building, New Square, Lincoln's Inn, London WC2A 3SB; Tel 0171 242 2523; fax 0171 691 1234.

Research and assistance by Gordon Lee LLB (Hons).

The Guide to the Convention Articles in Schedule 1 was written by David Pickersgill, a practising barrister at Bell Yard Chambers, 116-118 Chancery Lane, London WC2A 1PP; Tel 0171 306 9292; fax 0171 404 5143.

This publication is intended to be a brief commentary on the Human Rights Act 1998 and should not be relied upon by any party without taking further legal advice.

Index

Index compiled by Terry Halliday,
Indexing Specialists, Hove.